The Fathers and Sons of Deoband

Shaykh al-hadith Muhammad Zakariyya

© 2020 Madania Publications

PUBLISHER'S NOTE: Madania Publications is committed to making authentic publications of traditional Islamic scholarship available and accessible for the public benefit. Please contact us to acquire our books at special discounted rates for nonprofit purposes.

ISBN: 978-1-936157-13-6   1-936157-13-6

Book Design: A.J.
Translation and Annotation: Asim Ahmad
Front Cover Photo: Maaz's Photography (Shutterstock)
Final Edit: Mayada Osman
Typesetter: Annalisha Johnson

Cataloguing-in-Publication Data has been applied for and may be obtained from the Library of Congress.
Library of Congress: 2018934822
Distributed in USA by Darul Hikmah Bookstore

Printed and Bound in USA
10 9 8 7 6 5 4 3 2 1
Madania Publications

The front photo is an image of the Darul-Hadith complex at the main campus of Darul Uloom Deoband (Deoband, India).

May all the reward for this translated work go to my parents, my shaykh, and the Fathers and Sons of Deoband.

Other books translated/authored by translator

The Inseparability of Shari'a and Tariqat

Haj and Umra: The Epic Journey

Stories of the Sahaba ﷺ

Ramadan of the Elders

The Essentials of Jum'ua

Fathers and Sons
of Deoband

The *maslak* of the elders of Deoband has always remained that on which Imam-i-Rabbani Mujaddid Alf-i-Thani, Shah Waliullah Dehlawi and Shah 'Abdul 'Aziz were in that after hadith, with view of the importance of fiqh and ijtihad, the faqih of the Ummah, Imam Abu Hanifah, is accepted as imam and simultaneously the knowledge of the people of the hearts, the sciences of Tasawwuf and the sciences of purifying hearts is correctly blended; and if on the one side there is an acceptance of the great worth of Ibn Taymiyyah then, on the other, there is an admission of the achievements of Shaykh-i-Akbar Muhy al-Din Ibn 'Arabi.

Maulana Yusuf Binnori
(taken from Deoband.org)

These are my fathers, bring the likes of them
If you are going to gather the company, O Jarir!

Contents

Chapter Six

Chapter Seven

Translator's Note

The *Fathers and Sons of Deoband* is a lengthy letter disguised as a book and the culmination of an extended correspondence between the author, Shaykh ul Hadith Muhammad Zakariyya, and his son-in-law, Mufti Shahid. Mufti Shahid had been urging Shaykh ul Hadith to respond to an objection that was raised, it seems, by certain sectarian groups in the Subcontinent agitating against the people of Deoband. The two-pronged objection was: why do adherents of the Akabir of Deoband display a higher degree of reverence for their own Akabir over others, and why do they use one criteria for their own Akabir and another for everyone else?

The Response of Shaykh ul Hadith

This letter was written in 1398 A.H. (1978), exactly four years before Shaykh ul Hadith passed away. The major portion of his life had, to this point, been dedicated to hadith studies in one way or another. He had been teaching Bukhari for over forty years and Abu Dawud for thirty. He had authored innumerable books, volumes, and commentaries of various hadith texts, and had now disengaged himself from all his hadith preoccupations due to health factors. Though his pedagogical work and hadith research had come to a halt, he was now a world renowned muhaddith consulted by contemporary muhaddithun and students of hadith worldwide. Moreover, he was on a global mission for the past twenty years to revive the dhikr of Allah through the Chishtiyya line of Tasawwuf. His pedagogical and literary contributions in the field of hadith consumed most of his blessed life and saved him from engagement in the religious sectarianism that is rife in the Subcontinent to this day. As his lifetime of work attests, he was against any type of endeavors that may increase rift in Muslim unity, and as he himself asserts in the beginning of the letter, he considered it all absurdities and distractions from the essential purpose of Islam. This was the first of two reasons why he refused the urgent requests by his son-in-law to respond to this sectarian projectile. It is wholly possible that Mufti Shahid himself was under pressure to respond due to the controversy that had been stirred up by the objection at the time. Shaykh ul Hadith, on his part, had the insight to know that his rebuttal, no matter how truthful and convincing it may have been, would serve no purpose but to feed the appetite of a factious culture that thrives on sectarian divide.

The second reason to which Shaykh ul Hadith dedicates the bulk of this letter is the general principle of the Ahle Sunna wa al-Jama'a that all people cannot be judged by the same yardstick. The Auliya of Allah are the group within the Ahle Sunna who must be revered and whose actions and utterances interpreted in a way that corresponds to the Qur'an and Sunna. The reason for their privileged status is because they are a people that live, breathe, and die by the will of Allah and seek nothing from anything they say or do but the pleasure of Allah.

The Golden Principle About the Auliya Allah

Auliya is the plural of wali, which means friend. The wali of Allah is a friend of Allah, but not in the same sense as human friendship. This is why the translation of wali of Allah can be misleading. The wali of Allah, according to the hadith, is one who 'gives for Allah, refrains for the sake of Allah, loves for the sake of Allah, hates for the sake of Allah, and marries for the sake of Allah' (Tirmidhi). He is one who 'if he swears by Allah, Allah makes it happen' (Tirmidhi). Additionally, 'there are special ones of Allah whom He blesses with a life in *'afiya*,[1] and when He takes their life, He sends them to Paradise. When the *fitan* descend like a section of the pitch darkness of the night, this group will be in 'afiya from it' (al-Mu'jam al-Ausat).

Ibn Taymiyya, in his treatise about the Auliya of Allah in *al-Firaq Bayna Auliya' al-Rahman wa Auliya' al-Shaytan* explains that the two major characteristics of the wali of Allah are iman and taqwa. As evidence, he cites the ayah, 'listen, on the Auliya of Allah there is no fear, nor shall they grieve. Those who believed and feared Allah, for them are good tidings in his worldly life and in the Hereafter. No change is there in the words of Allah. That is what the great attainment is' (10:62-64). He further backs the ayah with the hadith *qudusi* in which Allah says, 'whoever turns against My wali, he has come to battle against Me—or I declare war on him—and My servant does not gain closeness to Me with anything as much as he does with fulfilling that which I have made compulsory upon him. And my servant gains closeness to Me with *nawafil* (supererogatory) prayers until I love him; and then when I love him, I become his ears by which he hears, his eyes by which he sees, his hand by which he grabs, and his feet by which he walks' (Bukhari).

Different Groups of Auliya of Allah

The Auliya of Allah are divided into many groups:

1. The greatest of the Auliya of Allah are the prophets of Allah. They are sinless from birth, immune to any thought of sin, big or small, and are living and breathing the name of Allah

night and day. They are the delegates of Allah who carry out the mission of propagating His message of the tauhid of Allah to their nations.

2. The Sahaba ﷺ are second in rank after the Prophets of Allah. The Sahaba ﷺ, unlike the Prophets, are not infallible, but have imbued the qualities and character of their Prophets to an extent that they too live, breathe, and die only for the sake of Allah. They are also delegates of Allah who uphold the mission of their Prophets. Regarding the Sahaba ﷺ, Imam Tahawi says in his treatise on the creed of the Ahl Sunna wa al-Jama'a,

> We love the companions of the Prophet ﷺ but not excessively [to the point of declaring them infallible], nor do we divorce ourselves from them; we despise those who despise them and speak ill of them; we do not remember them except with good; love for them is Deen, iman, and ihsan; malice toward them is disbelief, hypocrisy, and rebelliousness.[2]

In other words, because they are beloved to Allah and His Prophet ﷺ, they themselves are a criterion for determining a believer from a hypocrite. Those who love them, defend their honor, and revere them are true believers, while those who criticize them and refuse to accept the lofty status conferred on them by Allah and His Prophet ﷺ are misguided.

Ibn Taymiyya writes,

And of the [creedal] principles of Ahl Sunna are:

> They safeguard their hearts and tongues for the Sahaba ﷺ of the blessed Prophet. As Allah explains in the [translation of the] ayah, "And there is a share for those who came after them, saying, "Our Lord, forgive us and our brothers who preceded us in faith and put not in our hearts [any] resentment toward those who have believed. Our Lord, indeed You are Kind

and Merciful" (59:10). And obedience to the
Prophet in his narration, "Do not defame my
Sahaba for if you gave in charity the equivalent
of Mount Uhud in gold, it would not equal
even a mudd or half a mudd given in charity
by them."[3]

The bottom line that shapes the creed of the Ahle Sunna
about the Sahaba 🕮 as underlined by Imam Tahawi and Ibn
Taymiyya is that the fallibility of the Sahaba 🕮 cannot be made
a smokescreen for criticism of their mistakes. Indeed they were
fallible, but numerous ayah point out that Allah is pleased with
them as they are with Allah, and that they are forgiven. This
establishes an important principle, which we must know to
understand the third rank of Auliya: fallibility does not prevent
one from attaining the *wilaya* (sainthood) of Allah.

3. The third group of Auliya Allah are those who 'followed
them (i.e. the Sahaba 🕮) with good conduct' (9:100). This
group is also delegated by Allah for the work of Deen, but unlike
the Prophets and Sahaba 🕮, they will appear in every era. The
Prophet 🕮 said that, 'in my Umma, there will be a clique that
will remain until the Day of Judgment, undefeated and on the
Truth' (Muslim); and in another hadith, 'Allah will plant the
seeds in this Deen to whom He will use for His submission' (Ibn
Maja). The latter hadith suggests a strong similitude between
the Auliya and the Prophets in being raised by Allah under His
watchful eye, as He says about Musa 🕮, "That you might be
reared under My eye" (20:39).

Unlike the first group, which takes the name *Anbiya* or *Rusul*
in the Qur'an, and the second group *Sahaba, As-hab, Sabiqun,
Muhajirun,* and *Ansar,* and other similar appellations in the
Qur'an and Sunna, the third group is identified exclusively by
the generic term, Auliya Allah. Therefore, wherever the term
Auliya Allah is used out of the context of Prophets and Sahaba
🕮, it refers to this third group. For example, the ayah, "Listen,

the *friends of Allah* shall have no fear, nor shall they grieve. Those who believed and feared Allah" (10: 62-63), is used by Ibn Taymiyya for the third group, as cited above. Imam al-Mawardi and other mufassireen also explain this ayah in the same way. He says, "These are the people who 'have achieved His wilaya and are entitled to His honor'" (Tafsir al-Mawardi; 10:62).

4. The fourth and lowest rank of Auliya Allah are all those who profess faith in the *kalima*. They are the believers who are characterized by the full range of beautiful qualities that define a true believer. Allah says, "Indeed, the Muslim men and Muslim women, the believing men and believing women, the obedient men and obedient women, the truthful men and truthful women, the patient men and patient women, the humble men and humble women, the charitable men and charitable women, the fasting men and fasting women, the men who guard their private parts and the women who do so, and the men who remember Allah often and the women who do so: for them Allah has prepared forgiveness and a great reward" (33:35). Imam Tahawi says, "And the believers are all Auliya (friends) of Allah. And the most respected of them are the most obedient and those who follow the Qur'an most closely."[4]

The honor, rights, and reverence due to all four groups of Auliya Allah is proportionate to the order in which they are listed above. Without elaborating on the status of each in the ayahs and hadith, a few hadith on the status of the last group should suffice as it incorporates the rights and respect due to all four groups. The blessed Prophet ﷺ said, "A Muslim is one from whom another Muslim is saved from his tongue and his hands." "Defamation of a Muslim is *fisq* (major transgression) and to take his life is disbelief," and in Hajjat al-Wida', the blessed Prophet ﷺ delivered his parting sermon at Mina. One of the points he emphasized was, "Do not harm the Muslims and mock them and do not find faults in them. For he who finds faults in his Muslim brother, Allah will find his faults, and whomever Allah finds fault in, He will abase him even if it may be in the stomach of his mount," and that one should not harm a believer who has prayed his Fajr, for 'he is under the protection of Allah.' By hurting him, he is putting himself in harm's way with Allah (Muslim).

These prophetic exhortations prove that the believer is a wali of Allah. Never debase any wali of Allah since by doing so, one may be putting themselves in danger of divine retribution. Of most relevance to us here is that if these exhortations apply to the lowest rank of the Auliya of Allah, then what is to be said about the first three groups? An authentic hadith of Bukhari narrated about the third group is that he who debases the Auliya Allah, Allah has declared war against them. The declaration of war by Allah against a person simply means that there is nothing stopping from their destruction. It is also of significance that Allah does not declare war against anyone for any sin, minor or major, except for two: debasing the Auliya of Allah and the second, dealing in usury (2:279).

In this letter, Shaykh ul Hadith bases his whole argument against responding to sectarian objections on this Islamic principle and the personal conviction that we must revere the Auliya of Allah. He goes on to prove that the people of Deoband were Auliya of Allah and that we must imbue our hearts with reverence for them. To vilify them by criticism or objections, be it out of a secular mindset or sectarianism, is destructive. This is not to say that they are perfect, rather, any action or utterance seemingly out of line must be interpreted in a way that is befitting their status as Auliya of Allah and corresponding to the Qur'an and Sunna.

The first part of the letter elucidates the practice of past scholars toward seemingly objectionable utterings of the Auliya of Allah to prove that the Auliya of Allah must be judged on a different scale. He specifically cites Ibn Taymiyya, known for his hardline stance on issues, to represent the general consensus of scholarship. And yet, the manner in which he bends over backwards to interpret the controversial sayings of Shaykh 'Abdul Qadir Jaylani proves that though the Auliya of Allah are fallible, they should not be debased or criticized for what they say or do just because it does not sit well with our understanding of Deen.

The second and major part of this letter is the anecdotes from the lives of the Akabir of Deoband, in which Shaykh ul Hadith reminisces about the taqwa and piety of the Akabir. His sole objective of narrating these anecdotes is to prove that the Akabir of Deoband belonged to the third rank of Auliya of Allah, who should be revered and whose apparently objectionable actions and utterances must be interpreted. More implicitly, he is advising his son-in-law to realize that to respond to objections against the Auliya of Allah only substantiates the objectors and grants their objections credence. The best approach is the hands-off policy that is taken by all the Auliya of Allah, the *'Ibad al-Rahman*, in the face of ignorance. Allah says, 'And when the ignorant people speak to them, they reply peacefully' (25:63), and 'They will not hear anything absurd therein, but a word of peace' (19:62).

Change of Title

The published Urdu title of this book is not original, as it was neither chosen by nor attributed in any way to Shaykh ul Hadith. Being a letter of correspondence that was never intended for the public eye, the title is most probably a designation chosen by the publisher who converted the letter into book form. This helpful fact offers an alternative to change the title, which is advantageous to the purpose of the translation for several reasons.

The first of them is that the Urdu title of this letter is *Akabir Ulema Deoband,* which literally translates into 'The Elders of the Scholars of Deoband.' The problem with the word 'elders' is evident, as it denotes seniority in age, and whether the reader intends to or not, the mind gravitates toward the elderliness of the Akabir of Deoband. This defeats the objective of the book since the purpose of the ancedotes of the Akabir is to evidence their taqwa and iman and not their age, which is not a determinant factor of ranking in Islam whereas taqwa and piety are. Thus, the dissonance between the title and the content of this book defeats the unstated objective to increase our reverence for the Akabir.

But why rename it "Fathers and Sons of Deoband" and how is that a more fitting title for this book? A brief analysis of the father-and-son relationship, I think, would be the simplest way to understand this designation better.

The most obvious dimension of the father and son relationship is the hierarchy that is born out of the biological nature of the relationship. 'Elders' supposes a coeval relationship between the elders of Deoband. This can easily confuse readers unacquainted with a basic history of the Akabir, who may see them all as contemporaries, which they were not.

We notice the same father and son hierarchy in the Akabir of Deoband, literal in some cases and figurative in others. A literal example is of Shah Waliullah Dehlawi (1703-1763), the veritable father of Deoband, and his son, Shah Abdul Aziz (-1824); also Maulana Yahya Kandhelawi (1871-1917) and his son Shaykh ul Hadith Muhammad Zakariyya (1898-1982). The same form of figurative hierarchy, which is most common, we encounter between the Akabir in general.

The second dimension is the chemistry between a father

and son, which is a reciprocal relationship that is governed by fixed roles. The role of the father as the fosterer, breadwinner, and role model on one hand and the role of the son as a model of obedience on the other. We find that similitude in the relationships between the predecessors and successors in the Akabir. A simple example is the author's reverence for his shaykh, Maulana Khalil Ahmad Saharanpuri, and his shaykh's paternal-like affections and mentoring the spiritual growth and academic excellence of Shaykh ul Hadith.

The third and last dimension is the inheritance factor. A deceased father bequeaths assets and properties to the son. In the Akabir hierarchy, the successors also inherited the legacy of the Deoband vision from their predecessors.

Based on these correlations, the new title seems the most appropriate for this book. Furthermore, it clarifies any misunderstanding of who the Akabir were in terms of what made them beloved to Allah and His Prophet ﷺ.

A Last Word

Though a renowned muhaddith and a master of the Islamic sciences, our Shaykh al-Hadith's style of prose was surprisingly conversational and simple. His choice of words was straightforward and without complicated sentence structures or sophistication to how he communicated his thoughts. This is why his books were widely accepted among both scholars and the masses.

His simple prose was characterized by the occasional tangent, run-on sentences, and interpositions, which works well in Urdu but can be hard to keep up with in English. This is why I have taken considerable latitude in breaking sentences down and isolating interpositions between emdashes or placing them in footnotes to keep the flow. I have also avoided the diacritical marks that are common in academic works and papers since they constrain the conversational tone. Furthermore, the purpose of the book is not academic but spiritual excellence: to connect us with our tradition and our illustrious Akabir.

Also, I added bracketed and parenthetical comments where necessary to smooth out a sentence or clarify an unclear point. If the clarification is long enough to derail the reader, it has been put in the endnotes.

I have also added brief biographies of the Akabir which will help us better appreciate their taqwa and iman in light of the pillars of Islam.

The word Hazrat in Urdu is a title of reverence and is used frequently in the book. The context of the subheading will determine who the Hazrat refers to in the sentence.

I ask Allah to accept this book and make it a means of strengthening our connection with our Akabir.

CHAPTER ONE

Objections: Knowing the Limits

After the Sunna Salam,

My respected Maulvi Muhammad Shahid, may Allah protect him,

For many years, you have begged me to address the question:

Why are the scholars of Deoband so much in love with their Elders and why does it seem that they do not reserve the same love for any other [elder from a non-Deobandi line]? They even go so far as to draw hard-line fatwas of disbelief (*kufr*) against a person who utters something irrational, but then quickly cover it up with untenable interpretations after it is made evident that the statement is from the sayings of the Elders.

Despite your constant urging, I never took the objection seriously and refused to postpone my work and hadith studies to tend to such absurdities. I recall similar statements made by people in my childhood when I was about ten years of age, at the death of Maulana Rashid Ahmad Gangohi.[5] Shaykh ul Hind[6] composed a beautiful eulogy for Maulana Rashid Ahmad Gangohi which my father[7] printed and distributed in the thousands. I had memorized most of the eulogy and remember how I took great joy in reading it. I remember some people muttering about how we would be declared *kafir* if we had written this eulogy, but only because of its reputed author, no one will raise a voice against it.

I would often dispel such criticism by telling myself that such people are ignorant and not even worth the dirt that sticks to the sole of Shaykh ul Hind's shoes. What do they know about the profundity of his words? After that, I remember accompanying my father to Saharanpur when I was twelve. Other than the time he taught in the madrasa and when he went home to rest and sleep, he spent most of his time in the Mochiwala Masjid.

Objections Against People of Knowledge

The students in those days were truly exemplary. For them, serving their teachers was the greatest honor and they prided themselves over any opportunity to serve their teachers, unlike the 'enlightened students' of today who think their teachers owe their jobs and *roti*[8] to them.

It was summer time. My father was in the Mochiwala Masjid sitting by the well as two or three of his students lined up and poured buckets of water over him one after another. No sooner had one emptied his bucket that another stepped forward and emptied his bucket.

Hafiz Maqbul, the father of Maulvi Imdad, was among those who deeply loved my father and often came to the Mochiwala Masjid after Asr (to meet him there). He objected, "Shaykh, is this not wasting water?"

My father responded, "For you, but not for me."

Surprised, he asked, "What do you mean by that?"

My father explained, "Because you are unlearned and I am a Maulvi."

Hafiz Maqbul said, "But doesn't that support the stigma about Maulvis that they make everything permissible for themselves?"

My father replied, "Maulvis get annoyed for nothing by such accusations. The truth is that the Maulvi can make permissible (by his knowledge) that which is sinful by your ignorance."

He asked, "How is that?"

My father was curt. "Learn Arabic," he said.

You might remember my father's frequent claims about graduates from the British school system, especially lawyers and teachers, "If they gave me 72 hours, I could make Maulvis out of them all." And he was not bluffing. Many lawyers who had studied under him became almost full-fledged Maulvis in even less time than that.

Of course, my father never taught 72 hours straight; only two hours a week every Sunday. He loaded them with tons of homework which they were expected to complete by the upcoming Sunday. You might know one of the most famous solicitors of that time, Shihabuddin; and then there was Manfa'at 'Ali, who was head of the Muslim League[9] in the Saharanpur district, a *khalifa* (received authorization in Tasawwuf) of Maulana Ashraf 'Ali Thanawi,[10] and a very dear friend of mine. He also passed away after migrating to Pakistan. [Both of them studied under my father].

That was a tangent, but the point is that there were many such examples (of lawyers and other professionals) who [studied uner my father and] became Maulvis. In his introduction to *Ikmal al-Shiyam*,[11] Maulana 'Abdullah

Gangohi[12] praised my father's unique [and effective] method of teaching. At the time, Hafiz Maqbul and my father urged Maulana 'Abdullah Gangohi to learn Arabic for it would make him a [first-class] Maulvi.

I never really quite figured out the ruling about wasting water (which my father alluded to in the above dialogue between himself and Hafiz Maqbul) until I studied *Miskhat al-Masabih*[13] and came upon the hadith of Abu Sa'id al-Khudri ﷺ. He narrates that once Bilal ﷺ came to the Prophet ﷺ with high-quality *Barni* dates. The Prophet ﷺ asked him how he had acquired them.

He replied, "I bartered two *sa'a*[14] of low-quality dates for one sa'a of high-quality dates."

The Prophet ﷺ was appalled. He said, "Oh no! This is usury, this is usury! Never do such a thing; if you ever want to make a purchase, then sell it (i.e. the low-quality dates) for something else, and then buy it [i.e. the high-quality dates with the receipt from the sale of the low-quality dates]."[15]

I almost instantly recalled the bucket incident (and the conversation between my father and Hafiz Maqbul) in the Mochiwala Masjid, and now realized the meaning of the difference between a keeper of knowledge and an unlearned person. One could either barter a kilo of low-quality dates for two kilo of high-quality dates or, alternatively, sell the low-quality dates for one rupee and then purchase a lesser amount of high-quality date with that same rupee. On the surface, the result of both transactions seem identical, but the fact is that the unlearned person is conducting a usurious transaction while the Maulvi is not. Now it was clear to me, the same thing that could be permissible for a Maulvi could be impermissible for an unlearned person.

The first dean of our madrasa (seminary) in

Saharanpur, Maulana 'Inayat 'Ali, was a saintly and pious man. Perhaps, I have said a good word or two about him in my autobiography. He was a senior lecturer of hadith for two hadith classes but also served as head mufti (before the opening of the *ifta* department). Another one of his duties was collecting dues for the school. On his way to the madrasa, if he passed by the house or store of someone who defaulted, and the dues-collector had notified him that he had gone to collect the dues but they had not yet paid, he knocked on their door and said, "Oh my brother, we haven't received your payment yet." The poor defaulter would jump out of his chair in deference to him. Later that day, he would come around and pay his dues.

It was known that he always went to the market *himself* on his way to or from the madrasa to sell the jewelry he had collected for the dues. He made a point to never delegate this work to anyone. He did business with a famous money-exchanger who went by the name of Heera. Heera was very fond of Maulana and always gave him the best market value for his jewelry. Maulana was methodical about the way he conducted his business. Before selling the jewelry, he took a loan of silver coins from Heera. After he exchanged the jewelry and completed the transaction, he returned the silver coins and headed back home. Heera was deeply confused [by this peculiar practice] and wondered why Maulana took a loan of silver coins before the exchange and returned it immediately after the transaction was completed. Once, he decided to ask, "Maulana sahib! Why do you follow this custom and what does it mean? What difference does it make whether you take a loan or not?"

The dean explained that Islam has laid down very specific guidelines on doing business in gold and silver, and then went on to elaborate the juridical rulings of *sarf.*[16] Though he was a Hindu, Heera became so adept in the rulings of sarf that when any one of his Maulvi-like customers came along, he transacted with him until when the customer got up to go, he said, "Maulana sahib! Please be seated for a minute. It is forbidden in your religion to do business the way you just did." Most of the Maulvis would be flabbergasted. Others took exception and said, "Who do you think knows my religion better, you or I?" Heera was an old man. He gently replied, "Maulana sahib, please sit down; do not be angry with me and hear me out." Then he explained the Islamic method of doing business [in precious metals]. They would lose all their sureness, as they did not have a clue of what he was talking about while he was well-versed on the rulings of sarf.

[The point is that] The outcome of the transaction was the same according to both methods, but like the story of Bilal ☙ and his dates, the difference of a small adjustment converted an impermissible transaction into a permissible one.

Objections Against Sahaba ☙

In his book, *Miftah Dar al-Sa'ada,* Hafiz Ibn Qayyim says,

> But, one of the principles of Islamic law and of wisdom is that he who has many good and immense deeds to his name, and his influence on Islam is great, will be acquitted and forgiven more than others. Sin is a contaminant, and two containers of water can hold a contaminant better than a little water, for it cannot bear even a little. (We take this) from a hadith of the

blessed Prophet ﷺ in which he said to 'Umar ؓ, "Who knows, maybe Allah looked upon the veterans of Badr and said, 'Do what you like, I have forgiven you.'"[17]

And it was this same clemency [granted to the Sahaba ؓ of Badr] which prevented the blessed Prophet ﷺ from executing a man (Hatib bin Abi Balta'a ؓ) who was arrested before he could release sensitive information about the Prophet ﷺ and the believers to Quraysh. After his arrest, the Prophet ﷺ pardoned him only on the virtue of his being a veteran of Badr.

This incident points out that where there were grounds (treason) for passing the death penalty on him, Hatib's ؓ status as a veteran of Badr spared his life. In this case, his good deeds saved him from facing the consequences of an otherwise unforgivable crime.

Likewise, when the Prophet ﷺ exhorted the Sahaba ؓ to give charity to fund [the expedition of Tabuk], 'Uthman ؓ gave away a huge sum in charity. The blessed Prophet ﷺ announced, "From here on, 'Uthman may do whatever he wishes; no harm will come to him" (Tirmidhi).

Though Hassan bin Thabit ؓ was among those who accused 'Ayesha ؓ of wrongdoing, he still maintained his privileged status with the Prophet ﷺ, the Sahaba ؓ, and the Umma, only because he defended Islam and the blessed Prophet ﷺ with his powerful poetry. Even when 'Urwa bin Zubayr ؓ (the nephew of 'Ayesha ؓ) berated him (i.e. Hassan ؓ), 'Ayesha ؓ came to his defense and said, "He stood up for the Prophet ﷺ and defended him."

In another example, 'Ayesha ؓ spoke highly of Zaynab bint Jahsh ؓ despite her often strained relationship with her co-wife and even when it was most expedient for her to expose matters that would damage Zaynab's ؓ relationship with the Prophet ﷺ. But none of these expediencies ever prevented 'Ayesha ؓ from adopting a policy of total honesty about Zaynab ؓ, even to the extent of extolling her virtues. At one point, she said, "No one engaged me in vying for my position with the Prophet more than her, but I never saw anyone stronger in faith, more fearful of Allah, and striving harder to acquire the pleasure of Allah than her. Yes, she was short-tempered, but she was as quick to take charge over her emotions."

The Principle of Ayesha ؓ

It is better for us to adopt the policy of Ayesha ؓ and her student, Sa'id bin al-Musayyab,[18] who was the most learned about her rulings, which he codified in the principles of the science of *al-Jarah wa al-Ta'dil* (Critical Analysis of Narrators of Transmission). He said,

> There is no honorable person, scholar, or person of eminence without faults, but there are those whose faults should not be exposed; and thus, the faults of any such person whose good deeds outweigh his faults will be overlooked for the sake of his goodness.

Ibn Taymiyya Interprets Sayings of a Great Shaykh

The above principle was standard policy of the grandmasters (of the Islamic sciences), the *Salaf* (predecessors), and the *Khalaf* (successors) so that even scholars, such as Imam Ibn Taymiyya, went out of his way in his acerbic critiques to interpret the utterances of the

Auliya Allah [and vindicate claims against them]. In his collection of fatwas, he has interpreted the utterances of the great Sufis on myriad occasions, especially of Shaykh 'Abdul Qadir Jaylani.[19] In one place, he writes,

> "Love is a fire that destroys all but the desire of the beloved." Some misconstrue this quote by reasoning that since all that happens in the world is by the will of Allah, everything is worthy of being loved, be it disbelief or sin, because the apex of love [for Allah] is [belief in] that all that occurs [in the world] is by the will of Allah.... The true purport of the utterer by the words, 'the will of Allah,' is the will of Allah in relation to the pure and Islamic. So to paraphrase the saying: love is a fire that burns everything Allah dislikes. And the correct meaning is that the apex of love is that a servant desires only what Allah desires.[20]

In another place he writes,

> That the righteous shuyukh make such assertions as, "I see no one but Allah," means that I do not see anyone as my Sustainer beside Allah; and I do not assert anyone to be the Creator, Planner, and Worshipped one beside Allah; and also whenever I observe anything beside Him, I do not love nor fear it because the eye only sees that which it loves with its heart. The shuyukh never infer from this quote that whatever creation I see beside Allah are sustainers or creators of the heavens and the earth, because only he who is in deviance and decadent in the mind and belief, would mean such a thing.[21]

Shaykh ul Islam Ibn Taymiyya says,

> A second type of *fana* (self-annihilation) is unconsciousness of anything besides Allah. In such states of *fana,* a person may utter such things as, "I am the Truth, O My Glorified being; How great is my splendor and nothing is in this *jubba*[22] but Allah." Such ascriptions [and/or claims] are uttered in (rapturous) states when one loses consciousness of even the act of observation itself, towards the entity that is being observed, the experience of the presentness of the entity that is present, the act of remembering the entity that is being remembered, and the act of cognition of the entity that is being cognized. In such a *maqam* (spiritual station), he is in a state of unconsciousness in which the ability to distinguish is incapacitated, though he still savors the sweetness of iman.[23]

On another occasion, he says,

> Annihilate yourself from creation by the order of Allah; annihilate your own desires by His order and annihilate your will by His doing. When you achieve this state, you acquire the ability to become the vessel of the knowledge of Allah.

Note his commentary of the above *shat-hiyat* (lit. fantastical utterances),

> "The order of Allah" means to be removed from worship of and reliance on creation to worship of and reliance on Allah alone. So do not worship the creation in defiance of Allah, and do not hope to remove harm or gain profit from it; and annihilation of the desire and

will by the order and doing of Allah signifies complete submission to every order of the Shari'a and not to the whims of the self.[24]

Then he goes on at length to expound the esoteric meanings of the sayings of the Sufis, focusing extensively on correct interpretations of the (misconceived) utterances of Shaykh 'Abdul Qadir Jaylani.

In the same way, his devoted student, Hafiz Ibn Qayyim in *Madarij al-Salikin,* his commentary of *Manazil al-Salihin* by Shaykh ul Islam Harawi al-Sufi, provides an unending supply of interpretations for his utterances. He even went as far as to say that may Allah have mercy on Abu Isma'il (Shaykh ul Islam Harawi's agnomen) for opening the door of heterodoxy with his utterances by which heretics swore that he was from their camp, though he was not. Then he narrates one of his utterances, "Fana is that one becomes oblivious to and rejects everything beside the Truth in his knowledge and his state..."

He explains,

'Rejects everything beside the Truth,' does not mean that he is completely oblivious of existence but that the ingrainedness of everything beside Allah is false. Never was Shaykh ul Islam Harawi a pantheist; he was absolved from such an accusation, though it may be suspected from his utterance.[25]

In another place, he interprets the utterance, "Whichever sin people consider small is an enormity and whichever they consider an enormity is actually small."

If one deduces from this that the major and minor of sinfulness is rooted in the discernment of people, then this is false because people trivialize gazing at women, but consider fornication an enormity, and this indeed is the case (i.e. that gazing at women is a minor and fornication is an enormity). However, if one assumes that that which people trivialize because of their indifference is an enormity in the sight of Allah and that minor sin which is magnified to an enormity by fear of Allah is in reality a minor one because of that very fear of Allah [then that is correct]. The hadith indicate much the same because the Sahaba ﷺ saw many sins as destructive by virtue of their elevated status and closeness to Allah while those very sins were more trivial than a strand of hair for the successors who were of lower status and who varied among themselves [in status].[26]

Do Not Judge the Elders

My purpose of raising this topic is to show the necessity of subjective interpretation and exercising caution as hardline scholars have done regarding the utterances of those whose piety, taqwa, and adherence to the Shari'a is an incontestable fact.

To call this a bias in favor of one's own is a misconception and even a sign of ignorance itself. Every person occupies one rank or another and it is improper to randomly make interpretations for anyone or everyone. My perspective on the Elders of Deoband is that they were erudite and eminent scholars. There is no doubt in that they erred in their utterances [out of their humanness], but not everyone is of the position to be able to sift their utterances and find their mistakes. If someone were to note their words and present it to the mufti, he will draw a fatwa based on the apparent meaning since he is not required to investigate the identity of the utterer before giving his fatwa. Though, once he is made aware that this is the utterance of an elder, he is responsible for contextualizing the utterance and judging accordingly.

Anas ﷺ narrated in one hadith (about a repentant believer) that Allah is more pleased with the repentance of a servant than one among you who travels upon a camel carrying his provisions in a waterless desert. Then, his camel wanders off and is lost to the desert. Having lost all hope, he takes shade under a tree and prepares for death when suddenly, his camel appears before him. He takes hold of the camel's nose string and out of boundless joy proclaims, 'O Lord, You are my servant and I am your Lord!' He commits this mistake out of extreme delight.[27] So now, if someone was to take these words and seek fatwa that such-and-such person says, "I am your Lord and You are my servant," the mufti would have no recourse but to issue the fatwa of *kufr* against him, even though they were uttered in gratitude to Allah.

In another hadith, Abu Hurayra ﷺ narrated that the Prophet ﷺ said, "A man wasted his life (in sin) until when death came upon him, he instructed his sons, 'when I die, cremate me, crush my ashes, and throw them to the wind and sea. I swear by Allah, if He gets a hold of me, He will punish me like He has no other.' Thereafter, the sons followed through with his will after their father's death. Allah said to the earth, 'Bring out what you contain,' and there he was standing [in an instant].' Allah said, 'What led you to do this [i.e. to say what you said to your son]?'"

He replied, 'my fear of You, my Lord.' Thereupon, Allah forgave him.[28]

He uttered kufr out of fear of Allah, but was still forgiven by Allah. Thus, if the people of piety, knowledge, and taqwa utter something out of extreme grief or exultation, the mufti will issue a fatwa of kufr, but if he learns that it was uttered by a pious one, he will certainly make interpretations of it.

In my early years, I remember reading the story of the shepherd of Musa 🙵, which I enjoyed immensely. In my days, it came out as a book and sold for one or two *paisa*.[29] In summary, the story goes like this:

> Once Musa 🙵 saw a shepherd on the road who professed, "O Allah, where are You, so I can enslave myself to You, stitch your leather socks for You, and comb Your hair? Where are You, so I can serve You, sew and tailor Your clothes, wash them, pick Your fleas, and O *Muhtashim (the bashful one)!* I would serve You milk, and if You fell sick I would console You as I would my own. I would kiss and pamper Your baby hands and massage Your lovely cute feet. When it came time to sleep, I would brush down and smooth out Your cot; and if I saw Your house, I would serve You night and day with ghee and milk, and my job would be to serve the food and Yours to consume it. O the One for whom all my goats be sacrificed, and for whom I cry and wail out of my love for You!" The shepherd mumbled on. Musa 🙵 bade him to stop and asked, "Who are you talking to?" He replied, "To the One who created us and from whence the earth and sky came into being." Musa 🙵 said, "Oh, you fool! You fell into disbelief before you even believed (i.e. you uttered blasphemy before you even gained

knowledge of Allah). What is this profanity? Do stuff your mouth with cotton (i.e. keep your mouth shut)! The stain of your unbelief has soiled the world and your disbelief has tattered the silky clothe of Deen. If you refuse to shut your mouth, a divine fire will descend that will light the whole world on fire."

The shepherd said, "You have sewed up my mouth and struck me down with guilt (i.e. I never knew anything before this and uttered whatever came to mind out of my fervent love for Allah. Now that you rebuked me, I have learned something about Him, and realized that my utterances were irreverent. Now, I must keep silent and feel ashamed of what I said earlier)."

He shredded his clothe, heaved a sigh, lowered his head, and went on his way. The rebuke from Musa ﷺ further stoked his love for Allah because prior to it he only had love, and now he loved with some gnosis of Allah. Thus, as he heaved a heavy sigh and went into the jungle, Allah spoke to Musa ﷺ and said, "Why did you break off My servant from Me (i.e. he had achieved some level of closeness, but you pushed him away)? You have been sent to connect My servants to Me; so why did you cut him off? [Listen] We have created every human on nature (the natural state) and bestowed him with the language to express that nature. What seems like hymns of praise and honey for him is profanity and aloe to you….!"

In summary, we are speaking about pious and exalted

men who devoted [every breathe to] glorify Allah, unlike today's con-artists who disguise themselves as people of God (and utter blasphemies) without any intent to glorify Allah.

Anyhow, those who are intoxicated by their spiritual states should be left to their spiritual states, while those who are not, should be taught and guided within their capacities. We look at the inner and the spiritual state and not at the outward and the utterance. If a person flatters me but I know he is pretending and does not mean what he says, his praise will not please me in the slightest. But, if it pours from the heart with sincerity, though he may not articulate it properly, it will be accepted with Allah.

> O Musa, the knowers of the meaning of reverence and awe for Allah are the true shuyukh and the ones inebriated with spiritual states. Therefore, if a spiritually intoxicated person's speech is profane, he will be excused, though, only a wali of Allah may understand this and only when Allah has granted him the spiritual eye with which to recognize such subtleties. Therefore, it is important for the general public to stay away from such intoxicated people (*majdhubs*), since such people may be elevated in their own right, but are of little benefit to others.

> After the revelation, Musa ﷺ went searching for the shepherd in the jungle and eventually caught up to him. He said, "My brother, rejoice! You are free to say what you wish. There is no protocol of reverence for you; say what you please."

> Hearing this, the shepherd says, "Musa!

I am past that stage now; my heart has since sobered and I am no longer intoxicated (by my state). I have learned something about Allah from your rebuke and your flogging prodded my horse to gallop beyond its destination."

The story is long and something to enjoy for its sublimity and subtle meanings, which are analyzed and explained in *Kalida Mathnawi*. Nevertheless, the reason for narrating this story is to show that the travelers of the spiritual path of Sufism reach lofty states. If this is how it is, then their utterances must be reinterpreted. As for those who do not belong to this category, we will judge them by their outward. So, to conclude that this is a bias in favor of one's group or order is a fallacy.

Shaykh ul Islam Ibn Taymiyya has raised this topic in his fatawa on many occasions. In one place, he writes,

If the shuyukh are heard uttering such things that contravene the Shari'a, then in most cases it is falsehood attributed to them by deviants, and if it is authentically attributed to them, whatever correct interpretation can be given to it must be given.

In many places, he emphasizes the importance of interpreting the utterances of the shuyukh, as he himself has done on multiple occasions. He especially concentrates on the interpretation of the utterances of Shaykh 'Abdul Qadir Jaylani (of which I have cited a few examples above). This is why we interpret the utterances of our Elders of Deoband as other non-affiliates of Deoband have also done because we know them for their piety, austerity, taqwa, and adherence to the Shari'a.

CHAPTER TWO

Adherence to the Sunna of the Prophet ﷺ

Allah says in the Qur'an, "Say if you love Allah, then follow me, and Allah will love you, and will forgive you your sins. Allah is Forgiving and Merciful" (3:31).

According to various narrations in *al-Durr al-Manthur*, the reason for revelation of this aya was that many people claimed to love God. Allah responded with the criterion that no one can love Allah until they follow the Sunna of the Prophet ﷺ. Ibn 'Umar ؓ narrates from the Prophet ﷺ, "No one's faith can be complete until his desire is subservient to what I have brought."[30] In another hadith from Abu Darda, the Prophet ﷺ further explained, "Follow me in good deeds, taqwa, humility, and in subjugating the self."

Hasan al-Basri commented on this aya, "Love for Allah is adherence to the Sunna of the Prophet ﷺ."

Abu Rafi' ؓ narrates that the Prophet ﷺ said, "I should not see anyone leaning on a cushion, my enjoinder (*amr*) or interdiction (*nahiy*) is brought to his attention and he says, 'We do not know. We will only obey what is in the Qur'an.'"[31]

In *Miskhat al-Masabih*, Miqdam bin Ma'dikarab ؓ narrates that the Prophet ﷺ said, "Listen, I have been given the Qur'an and another along with it just like it (i.e. the Sunna). In our time, a gluttonous one will recline against his cushion and say, 'take the Qur'an only. Take its permissible as permissible and its forbidden as forbidden.' Even though, whatever the Prophet ﷺ declares forbidden is also forbidden in the Qur'an."

By 'gluttonous,' the Prophet ﷺ was alluding to the deviant statements of the like being the ill-effect of indulgent, secular societies. The poor and underfed rarely sound out such sacrileges. The same point is made in a similar hadith by 'Irbad bin Sariya ﷺ. The words are, "One among you reclines against his cushion and claims that Allah does not declare forbidden anything outside of Qur'an. Listen! I swear by Allah, I have also enjoined and advised and forbade many things. They are of the same importance as Qur'an, but in fact, even more." Again, "reclines against his cushion" conveys the same idea as "gluttonous" in the hadith before it.

The arrogant and vainglorious who indulge themselves under the roofs of mansions and are totally indifferent to the sacred knowledge like to ramble in this manner.

In another hadith by 'Irbad ﷺ, once the Prophet ﷺ led salat. Then he turned around and gave a moving talk that made the eyes tear and the hearts shudder. A man said, "Prophet of Allah, it is the talk of one who is ready to depart, so please advise us." The Prophet ﷺ said, "Hold on to my Sunna and the Sunna of my rightly-guided caliphs; avoid innovations in the Deen because every new thing is an innovation, and every innovation is a deviation" (Tirmidhi).

The Prophet ﷺ said, "Whosoever revives any one of my Sunna, which was abandoned after me, will receive the reward of those who act upon it without any reduction in their reward. And whosoever starts a new thing, which is disliked by Allah and His Prophet, will receive the sin of those who acted upon it without any reduction in their sin" (Tirmidhi).

Yet, in another hadith, he says, "This Umma can never unite on deviation, and the help of Allah is with the *jama'a* (community). Whoever separates from the jama'a will enter into the Hellfire." He also said, "Whoever revives my Sunna loves me, and he who loves me will be with me in Paradise" (Tirmidhi).

Abu Hurayra ؓ narrates that the Prophet ﷺ said, "Whoever acts upon my Sunna when my Umma is corrupted, will receive the reward of a hundred martyrs." Furthermore, he says in another hadith, "If Musa (ﷺ) was alive, he would follow me."

In a *mursal*[32] hadith from the *Muwatta'* of Imam Malik, the Prophet ﷺ said, "I am leaving two things with you; you will never deviate for as long as you hold on to them: the Book of Allah and the Sunna."

The Prophet ﷺ said, "Whoever honors an innovator has supported the destruction of the house of Islam." These few hadith taken from *Miskhat al-Masabih* highlight the importance of adherence to the Sunna.

Imam Ibn Shihabuddin al-Zuhri said, "Our Elders would say that salvation is in holding fast to the Sunna." Imam Malik said, "The Sunna is like the ark of Nuh; he who sits in it will be saved and he who does not will be drowned."

The yardstick of Islam by which everyone will be measured is adherence to the Sunna. The more one adheres to the Sunna, the closer and more beloved he is to Allah, even if he was never much of a progressive thinker.[33] And the further one is from the Sunna, the further Allah is from him, though he may be dubbed the 'Thinker of Islam,' 'Thinker of the World,' and 'Thinker of the Skies.'

Shaykh ul Islam Ibn Taymiyya said that the auliya of Allah must hold fast to the Qur'an and Sunna. None has the right to follow his heart unless it complies with the Qur'an and Sunna; this is a principle to which all the auliya of Allah agree. Whoever opposes this is not from the auliya of Allah. He is either a disbeliever or just plain ignorant. The shuyukh have elaborated on this point in their works. For example, Shaykh Abu Sulayman al-Darani[34] said that I feel the descent of spiritual meanings upon my heart, but never accept them without two witnesses (Qur'an and Sunna). Junayd al-Baghdadi[35] said that this knowledge of ours (of Tasawwuf) is inseparable from the Qur'an and Sunna. Whoever has not studied the Qur'an and Sunna, cannot speak with authority on the subject of Tasawwuf. Abu 'Uthman al-Naysaburi said that he who subordinates himself to the Qur'an and Sunna in his words and deeds will compose words of wisdom; and he who subordinates himself to his desires will fall into innovation. This is because the Qur'an says: *And if you follow him, you will be guided...* Ibn Nujayd said that every spiritual state unsubstantiated by the Qur'an and Sunna is falsehood. In another place, he says that Fudayl bin 'Ayad[36] said that until the deed is not sincere and good it will never be accepted. By 'sincere', we mean that the action is for Allah alone and by 'good' we mean it is according to the Sunna.

Abu Sulayman al-Darani said that one should not act upon any good thought that descends upon his heart until he finds *athar* (proof from the Sunna) for it. Once the proof is provided, it is light upon light. Sahl bin 'Abdullah al-Tustari[37] said that any deed that is borne out of innovation is a punishment upon the self, and the deed which does not submit to the way of the elders is deception of the self.

Shaykh ul Islam Ibn Taymiyya and others narrate many similar utterances that prove that any deed not complying with the Sunna is deviation.

Elders of Deoband and the Sunna

Now, put aside rancor and obstinacy (toward the Elders of Deoband) and look at how rigorously they held fast to the Sunna. There is not enough room to cover the many stories of their adherence to the Sunna in the biographies and voluminous books, let alone in this letter.

Maulana Rashid Ahmad Gangohi

It is Sunna to step out of the masjid with the left foot first and to wear the right shoe first. In regards to the habit of Shaykh Maulana Rashid Ahmad Gangohi, numerous narrations mention, and I have witnessed it for myself, that when he came out of the masjid, he stepped out with the left foot, which he placed *on* the shoe or sandal, then stepped out with the right foot, slipped it into his shoe or sandal, and only after that wore his left shoe or sandal.

Once a person came, and the story is long, but shaykh had gone to the bathroom. When he returned, the person greeted him saying, "*Janab Adab* (lit. Sir, my respects!)."[38] Shaykh was angry and said, "Who is this inconsiderate man, so ignorant of one of the proprieties of the Shari'a?"

A person once came and said, "Hazrat, *salamat!*" His face flushed with anger as he replied, "The greeting of Muslims is essential here! What is this 'Hazrat, salamat'?"

In his will, he advised, "My wife, children, and my friends are advised to imbue the Sunna of the Prophet ﷺ which is necessary for adhering to the Shari'a. Consider even a slight contravention of the Sunna the worst enemy."

Shaykh ul Hind

Shaykh ul Hind's [daily] routine was to pray two *rak'a* in a sitting position after his witr. One of his students inquired, "Shaykh, the reward is halved for praying in a sitting position." Shaykh replied, "I know this to be true brother, but praying two rak'a in a sitting position after witr is established by the Sunna."

It is said of Shaykh ul Hind that his most devoted attendants, those who had served him for long, could not recall the slightest lapse in his adherence to the Sunna, let alone a word or deed against the Shari'a. Whether day or night, sickness or good health, on journey or at home, in public or private, he was always conscious of following the Sunna, and constantly encouraged his students, in every possible way, to do the same.

The Sunna was second nature to him. Each Sunna was performed solemnly and with natural ease, but at the same time, he was never one to start quoting hadith to prove or make himself revered by others. When the first fruit of the season was offered to him, he would smell its fragrance, put it to his forehead, and then called for a child and gave it to him; he hid his acting upon the hadith of *'ahdi bi rabbihi*[39] by saying that he was checking to see if the rain had stopped, and then rubbed the raindrops over his face and hands.

Mian Asghar Hussayn[40] narrates that Shaykh ul Hind

heard I was sick and came to visit me. He shook my hands and turned around to leave. I retorted, "Was this the only day you could find to act upon the hadith?" Shaykh ul Hind smiled and narrated the hadith, *the visit to the sick should be the duration between two milkings* (i.e. short).[41]

'Eid ul Adha came upon Shaykh ul Hind while he was a political prisoner [of the British]. He was detained in Malta where Muslim detainees were [under constant surveillance and] strictly banned from carrying out their religious duties. Now, sacrificing an animal in 'Eid ul Adha is not even mandatory upon a traveler, but Shaykh ul Hind was not to be deterred by any of that. He protested with the warden to be provided with sacrificial animals. In India, Shaykh ul Hind sacrificed many animals every Eid and was very passionate about upholding this Sunna. [It is said that] Anything that comes from the heart never goes unheard. The warden and other jail officials were so impressed, they bought him a sacrificial animal for seven guinea,[42] which the shaykh most happily paid for. The Sunna of Ibrahim ﷺ was most likely revived for the first time in this *Dar al-Kufr* since the downfall of the Ottoman Empire. On the 10th of Dhul Hijja, shaykh said the takbir in a loud voice and sacrificed his animal. He showed that where there's a will, there's a way; then even desirable acts can be carried out in the most inconceivable circumstances.

The hadith states that vinegar is the best dish. If it was placed on the mat, he took the greatest liking towards it and sometimes even took a gulp or two.

Once, his body broke out in blisters and the doctors advised him against consuming vinegar, but he still took some [to follow the Sunna].

Shaykh ul Hind married all four of his daughters in exactly the same way his teacher, Maulana Qasim

Nanautawi, would have liked, in the typical Sunna fashion and without any show or pretension. On the wedding of one of his daughters, he made an announcement after salat in the Jamiʿ Masjid, called for his future son-in-law, and solemnized the *nikah.* On another occasion, he read the Sunna *khutbah* and solemnized the nikah in a gathering of students and teachers of the madrasa. When he saw his daughter off, she was dressed in the plainest clothes and was seated in the plainest, most outdated palanquin. It only befitted the greatest muhaddith of his time and a lover of the Sunna to do things in this way.

Maulana Hussayn Ahmad Madani

The anecdotes about Maulana Hussayn Ahmad Madani's[43] scrupulousness in matters of Sunna are legendary, and there are still many who can bear witness to this, but there are far too many stories than can be covered in this letter. This abject one[44] has observed two shuyukh from the Elders who sobbed more than they cried at *tahajjud* time; one, my father, and the other, Shaykh ul Islam Maulana Hussayn Ahmad Madani. They convulsed when they sobbed like a child after he gets a beating. Qari Muhammad Mian, a teacher at the Madrasa Fatahpuri, narrates:

> In tahajjud, he [i.e. Shaykh ul Islam Maulana Hussayn Ahmad Madani] started with two short rakʿa followed by two long rakʿa in which he recited one and a half to two juz of Qur'an. He recited loud enough that a person sitting nearby would be able to hear the recitation if he put his ear to it. There would

be so much convulsing and shuddering during the recitation and his chest would be heaving great sighs. It is said about the Prophet ﷺ in tahajjud, *when he would pray, a sound like the boiling of a kettle emitted from within because of his crying.* I have witnessed such a state with my own eyes. After tahajjud, he (i.e. Shaykh ul Islam Maulana Hussayn Ahmad Madani] would make du'a and then sat in his place of prayer to make *istighfar* with the *tasbih* in his hand, a handkerchief in front, and a cuspidor at his side. On countless occasions, I saw the powerful scenes of his sobbing, which I never saw at any other time. He continuously wiped away the constant flow of tears with his handkerchief and rocked back and forth and side to side repeating *Astaghfirullahalladhi la ilaha illa huwa al-Hayy al-Quyyum wa Atubu ilayh* (*I make istighfar to Allah beside whom there is no deity. He is the Living, Self-Subsisting, and I repent to him*). Sometimes, he would recite other dhikr. On occasion, he would even recite Persian or Urdu poetry in his broken and humbled state.

I heard him chanting many Hindi couplets at this time. Mufti Mehdi Hassan says:

> His fervor for worship was so intense that even with a high fever, he recited long Suras (*al-tawal al-mufassal*) in Fajr. As for Sunna, he sought out a Sunna in everything, no matter how little it seemed to relate to the Sunna. The world was amazed to know that an Acacia tree was planted in the main square of Darul 'Ulum Deoband. People thought, "What is the benefit

of a tree that bears no fruit nor flowers. It is neither picturesque nor adds any luster to the garden. Then why was it planted?" Later, they learned it was planted as a memorial to the Pledge of Ridwan, which the Prophet ﷺ took from the Sahaba ﷺ under an Acacia tree of the same family.

Maulana Khalil Ahmad Saharanpuri

While the work on *Badhl*[45] and the hadith of *naza'ir*[46] in Abu Dawud (which opposes the order of Suras in the Mus-haf 'Uthmani) came under review, my shaykh (Khalil Ahmad Saharanpuri[47]) said to me, "Note this hadith and give it to me. I will recite it in tahajjud tonight."

In their devotion to the Sunna, the Elders never worried about gaining less reward, as my father once said, "Attending the call of nature according to the Sunna is more rewarding than optional salat against it."

Maulana Rashid Ahmad Gangohi (2)

Maulana 'Ashiq Ilahi Mirat-hi, the biographer of Maulana Rashid Ahmad Gangohi, writes,

> The firm-footedness of the shaykh in the Sunna, better known as *istiqama* (steadfastness), was so transparent that to bring proof for it would be like showing a lantern to the sun. There are many who love the Sunna, but rare are those whose love for the Sunna has permeated the recesses of the heart, which is better

translated as *fana'iyyat* or self-annihilation (i.e. the habits and traits of the self are completely annihilated and replaced by the character of the Sunna). The sign of achievement of this (most extraordinary) level is that one does not, even forgetfully (or even reflexively), commit any act that opposes the Sunna.

Maulvi Hakim Muhammad Isma'il Gangohi Ajmeri wrote an ode (*qasida*) in praise of his shaykh (Maulana Rashid Ahmad Gangohi) and read it out (in his shaykh's gathering), even while the shaykh admonished him. (Emboldened) By the shaykh's affections for him, he continued to read on. When he finished, shaykh lowered his head and then took up a handful of dirt and threw it on him. Hakim Ishaq protested, "Shaykh, my clothes have become dirty!" He replied, "This is the recompense for praising one in his presence. What can I do? It is the order of the Prophet ﷺ."[48]

Maulana Khalil Ahmad Saharanpuri

In the biography of Shaykh Khalil Ahmad Saharanpuri, Maulana 'Ashiq Ilahi Mirat-hi writes:

Once, the shaykh was in Mina (during the days of hajj). Baggages and belongings lay in heaps around the howdahs everywhere. Suddenly, the *mutawwif* (hajj guide) came around before dawn and announced, "Be ready to depart for Arafat!"[49]

What do I see but the shaykh nestled in a narrow pathway between two howdahs. He was standing and calmly reciting Qur'an, oblivious to his surroundings. The hajj and camel guides both were agitating to move, but the shaykh did not shorten his tahajjud by even a single ayah. After making the *salam*, his face became red with anger and he spoke sharply to the hajj guide, "Have you forgotten the deal we made that we would only perform the hajj according to the Sunna and you agreed to abide by our wishes! Then what right do you have to hurry us and force us to depart before sunrise?"

The guide said, "What am I to do? The camel guides listen to no one and follow only their whims. If they tromp off with the camels, the whole hajj will come to a standstill. It is not a good idea to miss the obligatory of hajj for the sake of the Sunna."

The shaykh was even more incensed. He charged, "You should know that we hired you as a hajj guide and not a shaykh to advise us! Go and tend to your business because we have no mind to leave even a minute before sunrise. We spend our (hard-earned) money and bear all the hardships of the hajj journey so that we can complete our hajj according to the Sunna and not to be enslaved to you and your camel guides. They can go ahead and do whatever suits their fancy with their camels. They can tromp off with their camels if they like, but we are under no obligation to follow their lead. You raised this hue and cry for nothing and needlessly disturbed our salat. [Go] I free you of your obligations to us! Go take care of the other hajis and leave us alone. By the grace of Allah, we are not lame, and Arafat is not all that far. If the camels depart, we will, inshallah, arrive at Arafat on foot. But, if you want us to abandon the Sunna and do as you say, then expect nothing from us!"

Once, one of his students tried to plead a case for a respected scholar [who was a relative of the shaykh and whom the shaykh had denounced] from the Rahtak District and said, "Shaykh! He is your family and one of our own.

He only disagrees on some minor issues of belief, which happened even with some of the Imams of the past..." He had barely started his argument when an incredulous look came across the shaykh's face, and he said, "What! Disagreement, and on matters of belief? You yourself admit that he holds a difference of opinion on some lesser beliefs. As far as I am concerned, even if he held no opinion, but entertains a doubt, he is in deviation. And then, how audacious of you to rationalize his difference of opinion by comparing it to the predecessors! One can falter in good deeds, but if, God forbid, any Muslim takes an innovation for a Sunna or questions whether a Sunna is even Sunna, he is destroyed."

He carried a miswak in his *kurta* or pillowcase, even while on journey, and never performed *wudu* (ablution) without the miswak.

Shah Isma'il Shahid

It is narrated about Shah Isma'il Shahid,[50] in the book *Arwahe Thalatha*,[51] that one small area of the front row of the Akbari Masjid[52] caved in and turned mucky [when it rained]. Worshippers avoided that area by standing in the second row instead. But, the shaykh (Shah Isma'il Shahid), who in those days took a liking for fine clothes, would come and stand in that very area (whereby his clothes would sometimes get soiled). He did this only out of his desire to follow the Sunna [i.e. to complete the first row before starting the second].

When taking bay'a (pledge) from anyone, he always emphasized strict adherence to the Sunna. He once said to Maulana 'Abdul Hayy Lakhnawi, "Let me know if you ever observe me doing anything against the Sunna." Maulana 'Abd al-Hayy replied, "Do you think 'Abdul Hayy will remain in your company if he ever observes you opposing the Sunna?"

Maulana 'Abd al-Hayy's vigilance towards his shaykh's adherence to the Sunna sometimes called for admonishment. Once, Syed Ahmad Shahid, who had just married, came past his usual time for salat. Maulana 'Abdul Hayy took notice but let it pass on the first day. On the second day, Syed Ahmad Shahid missed the *takbir ula* (the first takbir of salat). Maulana 'Abdul Hayy made the salam and said, "So what will it be, the worship of Allah or celebration of marriage?" Syed Ahmad Shahid immediately admitted his mistake [and vowed to never do it again].

Maulana Isma'il Kandhelawi

Amir Shah Khan wrote of my grandfather, Maulana Isma'il of Nizamuddin,

> Whenever I met him, he would say, "The hadith says that whenever you meet someone you love, you should let them know. Out of my submission to this prophetic order, I say to you, 'I love you.'" This was his perpetual habit throughout his life without exception.

In his commentary, Maulana Ashraf 'Ali Thanawi writes, "His zeal for the Sunna forced him to repetition, otherwise, saying it once [i.e. that he loved someone] was enough."

In another incident about my grandfather:

> He once said to Shaykh Rashid Ahmad

Gangohi in private, "I have made bay'a with Maulana Muhammad Ya'qub Dehlawi and was instructed by Maulana Muzaffar Hussayn from the Naqshbandi order. After following their Sufi prescriptions for a few days, my six *lata'if* [53] came to life, but as I always loved the Sunna, I recited the various prophetic supplications for different occasions, the du'a for entering and exiting the bathroom and the du'a for entering the marketplace. I am extremely diligent in my reading of these supplications, which is why I never took much interest in the Sufi prescriptions of the shuyukh. I would meditate once every ten to fifteen days, at most. This is my present situation, but presently, I am old and weak. I wish that you would prescribe me something to do."

Maulana Rashid Ahmad Gangohi explained, "You have achieved the level of *ihsan*[54] in your present routine (i.e. through prophetic supplications) and are not in need of any Sufi prescriptions. But if you did, you would be regressing like a person who has studied *Bostan* and *Gulistan* going back to *Karima*.[55] For you to apply the Sufi prescriptions and litanies is a waste of time and a sin."

I have heard another variant of this story, which replaces the examples of *Bostan* and *Gulistan*. It is as follows:

That would be like someone making a request to be taught the primer on the Arabic alphabet, *Qa'ida al-Baghdadi*, after already knowing how to recite Qur'an and saying, "Teach me the *Qa'ida al-Baghdadi*; I have never read it."

Maulana Qasim Nanautawi

In a famous incident about Maulana Qasim Nanautawi, after the Uprising of 1857,[56] it is narrated that when the British put a bounty on his head, his well-wishers and the Muslim community forced him into hiding. He came out on the third day and said, "Evidence shows that the Prophet ﷺ hid in the Cave of Thawr for only three days."

His biographer quotes him in *Sawanih Qasmi* as saying, "A customer hands a tailor a shirt and tells him, 'make a shirt identical to this one.' Now, the closer the tailor replicates the sample shirt, the more entitled he is to full compensation for his work." He used this metaphor to say, "The *uswa hasana*[57] (good example) of the blessed Prophet ﷺ is the sample we have been given by Allah. Human beings must fashion themselves on his way, conduct, and his outlook on life. The more one follows his example, the more beloved he will be to the Beloved (i.e. Allah)."

In another incident from *Sawanih Qasmi*:

Once, returning from a long journey to his hometown of Nanauta, he stayed in the masjid for a short while and prayed *nafl* (optional prayers). When the locals learned of his arrival, they rushed to the masjid to meet him.[58]

Critics should find the likes of the Elders of Deoband in their adherence to the Sunna of the Prophet ﷺ. Indeed, they will be hard-pressed to find anyone who followed the Sunna in his/her sitting, standing, eating, drinking, and the such as the Elders of Deoband did.

Ibadat and the Four Pillars of Islam

Now, listen further! Islam rests on four pillars, or the *'ibadat* (acts of worship) i.e. salat, fasting in Ramadan, zakat, and hajj. The mass-authenticated hadith refer to these four pillars as the foundations of Islam. The muhaddithun and fuqaha (jurists) have traditionally employed this term ('ibadat) to define the four pillars of Islam the way the Prophet ﷺ did in many hadith. But, many free-thinkers of our time say that salat, fasting, zakat, and hajj are but a training course for the true and real 'ibadat.[59] They say that these 'ibadat are only to train us for 'higher 'ibadat,' as if to say that no one, including the Prophet ﷺ, was enlightened to the true meaning of 'ibadat until they came along.

(In the famous hadith of Jibril ﷺ) Jibril ﷺ came to teach the Prophet ﷺ about the Deen and inquired about the meaning of Islam. The Prophet ﷺ responded by narrating the four pillars of Islam, which Jibril ﷺ affirmed. [It seems as though] Neither Jibril nor the Prophet ﷺ were enlightened about the higher meaning of 'ibadat. Numerous hadith state that these four pillars are the foundation of Islam, but I have never come upon any hadith stating that these four 'ibadat were a 'training course' to achieve a higher objective.

Once, a bedouin came and asked the Prophet ﷺ, "Tell me some deed by which I may enter Paradise." The Prophet ﷺ taught him the four pillars. He said, "Prophet of Allah! I will do no more or less than this." The Prophet ﷺ said, "Whoever likes to see a dweller of Paradise, should look at him."

Whatever we know from the Qur'an and Sunna and the tradition of the Salaf is that 'ibadat refers to those acts of worship that are traditionally defined as the pillars (*arkan*) of Islam, which is by consensus [of the Umma], the road to salvation.

[It should be understood that] Though many supplementary acts are called 'ibadat, it is only because they are conducive to establishing the pillars of Islam. There are many devotional acts that are virtuous deeds and are called 'ibadat, but only figuratively, since they promise abundant reward in the Hereafter (like the four pillars).

Some modern-thinkers in the present times relegate the four pillars, disregard the definitions given by the Qur'an and Sunna, and have already formulated their own definitions of 'ibadat, which is a major cause of deviation. The outcome can be noticed in the interpolations you will find in the writings and speeches of their followers, which is most certainly injurious to the faith. Many who do not have a strong base in Deen are misled by their literature.

May Allah save the Umma from every type of innovation and interpolation. May He allow us to understand and adopt the Deen as it was revealed and understood by the Prophet ﷺ and his first devout followers, the Sahaba ﵃, who transmitted the words and meanings most faithfully to the Former (Salaf) who passed it on to the Latter (Khalaf), who transmitted it to us; this transmission will continue uninterrupted through the passage of time until the Day of Judgment. *And Allah is in control of His situation, but most do not know.*

In reality, the main reason for such ideological distortions in our time is the liberal mindset, which is the outcome of self-study of religious books without a solid and basic understanding of the Deen.

I remember a story from childhood about a conceited seeker of knowledge who said, "What is the need for teachers and why must you learn from someone? All you need is to study the books of the curricula."

He started studying Persian and came upon this poem by Sa'di,

سعدی که- گوئے- بلا

Sa'di kih goi' bala

گت ربود -در ایام

gat rabud dar ayyam

بو بکر بن سعد بود

bu Bakr bin Sa'd bud

[Dissection of the poem:] *Sa'di* was Sa'di and he already knew the meaning of *goi'* (ball). He picked up on the subtle figurative in, *Sa'di took the ball of bala* (tribulation), but got stuck on the meaning of *gat rabud*. He searched and searched, but came up with nothing. It was not to be found in any lexicon nor any book. From thereon, *gat rabud* became an expression to mean garble (unintelligible words).

It is narrated in a hadith from *Majma' al-Bihar*:

نُهِيَ عَنِ الْحِلَقِ قَبْلَ الصَّلَاةِ اَيْ صَلَاةَ الْجُمُعَةِ

The Prophet ﷺ prohibited halaq/hilaq before salat i.e. Jumu'a salat.

Hilaq is the plural of *halaqa,* which means study-circle. Some ignoramuses read it as *halaq* (shaving of the hair) and never shaved their head before Jum'ua for the next 40 years.

These are the follies of self-study, even though other transmissions of this hadith elaborate upon this wording of the hadith with the word *tahalluq* (to sit in a circle).

It is narrated in the *Shama'il* of Tirmidhi that Imam Ibn Sirin said, "Hadith is of the Deen, so before you seek [the knowledge of hadith], know who you are acquiring your Deen from." In the *Shama'il*, it is mentioned that Ibn Sirin was the imam and famous *tabi'i* (successor) of his time who learned from countless Sahaba 🙏. He was also the authority on the Science of Interpretation of Dreams.

What Imam Ibn Sirin meant was that you must carefully examine the character, taqwa, school of thought, and the beliefs of the prospective teacher and should not just take what everyone says about him, regardless of his deficient character and impiety. [Remember] All that will rub off on you... Sometimes we are naive because of the adage: 'you should look at what is being said and not who is saying it.' That is essentially true, but only for he who understands and can distinguish between truth, falsehood, and an error. As for those who lack understanding of the Deen and cannot distinguish between genuine and counterfeit, truth and false, and right and wrong, they should not accept everything they hear from everyone. The result of such naiveté leads to harm and injury in the Deen. This is why every claimant to sainthood, *mujaddidiyyat* (revivalism), prophethood, or even Godhood attracts a large crowd in our times.

In Bukhari, the Prophet 🙏 said, "Knowledge is seeking." The hadith commentators narrate this specific hadith with many chains of transmission. Ibn Hajar al-'Asqalani commented, "The meaning of this [hadith] is that only knowledge that is sought from the prophets and their inheritors is authentic."

In Bukhari, the Prophet 🙏 said, "Allah will not erase knowledge by lifting it from the hearts of the people all at once. But, He will remove the [sacred] knowledge by taking away the scholars until no [authentic] scholars remain. Then, people will appoint ignorant people as their guides. People will inquire from them and they will issue fatwa without knowledge; they will be misguided and will misguide others."

We are observing this phenomenon in our time. When an authentic scholar passes away, he vacates his position that should be, but is not, presently being filled by a scholar of equal repute, let alone one of a higher one. As a result, the community hires ignorant people as their imams and leaders. The Prophet 鷺 announced in Hajjat al-Wada'a, "Seek the knowledge before it is taken away."

Someone asked, "Prophet of Allah, how will the knowledge be taken away?"

He replied, "By the removal of its messengers (i.e. scholars)." He repeated this three times.

CHAPTER THREE

Salat

Salat is the most sacred of all 'ibadat, and the first we will be reckoned for on the Day of Judgment. The Prophet ﷺ said, "Fear Allah regarding the salat, fear Allah regarding the salat, fear Allah regarding the salat! The difference between a believer and disbeliever is the salat."

Salat is the symbol of Islam. Whoever puts his heart into salat and prays it in the best way, fulfilling all the *mustahab* (desirable) and Sunna, is a true believer. Allah never chose anything greater than iman and salat. Had there been, it would have been assigned to the angels. Night and day, some angels are in *ruku'*, while others in prostration. Salat is the pillar of Islam and the greatest struggle. And when divine retribution is about to strike, it is the masjid-goers who are saved [by virtue of their salat].

I am narrating some incidents about salat in the lives of the fathers and sons of Deoband but have not ensured I cover every aspect of it in their lives, as that would require a book in and of itself.

Maulana Rashid Ahmad Gangohi

It is narrated in *Tadhkirat al-Rashid* that Maulvi Mumtaz 'Ali Anbetawi narrated that Maulana Abul Khayr was in Baluchistan (province in Pakistan) when news reached of Maulana Rashid Ahmad Gangohi's passing away. He sent for me twice to come and meet him. When I finally arrived, I found him crying profusely. The moment he saw me, his condition worsened. He lost control and sobbed until it could be heard all around. Everyone in the gathering was shaken and it seemed as though everyone would fall unconscious. Then, he (Maulana Abul Khayr) finally spoke and said, "Ah, Maulvi Mumtaz 'Ali! A great personality has passed on from the Subcontinent. It is so disheartening to see that people did not recognize his caliber. I have heard from countless reliable sources that the shaykh would cry the whole night over a single ayah, and that ayah was:

$$\text{يَوْمَ تُبْلَى السَّرَائِرُ فَمَا لَهُ مِنْ قُوَّةٍ وَلَا نَاصِرٍ}$$

The Day when all the secrets will be examined (as to their truth). Then will (man) have no power, nor any helper (86: 9-10).

It is written elsewhere that the magnificence of Allah permeated his every vein and pore. During recitation of Qur'an, a state would overcome him, which became more evident when no one was around. In the last part of the night, in a quiet and empty house, he would stand before his Lord in solitude and recite in *nawafil*. Quickly, he broke down crying and was forced to pause repeatedly during the recitation. He choked on his tears and often went silent, trying to control the urge to sob. Tears flowed down his cheeks and into his beard soaking the prayer mat on which he prayed.

Maulvi 'Abdul Rahman Khaurjawi says: once, I came to Gangoh in the month of Ramadan. Shaykh would lead the salat in *tarawih*. One night, he started tarawih, and I was there at the time. He continued reciting until he reached a part in which Allah exhorts mankind to fear Him. Less than half the congregation knew Arabic, the rest were completely unlearned. His fear of Allah manifested in the recitation, which shook up the whole congregation. Some were crying, while others were shuddering. When he started the next few passages about the mercy of Allah, the ambience suddenly changed and the congregation was now jubilant; some could not even contain their laughter.

Of his prudence in personal affairs, it is known that he always relied on the most preferred and reserved opinion on issues of differences of opinions. Despite need or necessity, he never forsook prudence. The smallest example of this is how he adamantly refused to sit down and pray, even when he was extremely sick. In the days before his death, two or three people from both sides propped him up with their hands behind his back. He prayed the whole salat standing, bowing, and in prostration with the attendants' assistance. How often the attendants entreated him to sit and pray, but he never gave it thought or even bothered to respond to their requests. One day Maulvi Yahya said, "Hazrat, you are not obliged to sit in a standing position, and when exactly is the time to take the dispensation if not now and in this state?" He replied, "In the opinion of Imam Abu Hanifa, he who can worship by the help of others is considered able, and when I have friends who assist me in standing up and praying, then how can I pray in a sitting position."

But when his health deteriorated and he could no longer stand, even with the help of his attendants, he prayed *some* of his salat in a sitting position.

Hazrat Gangohi suffered a cataract in the last few years of his life. The attendants pressed him for surgery but he refused. One surgeon promised he would not allow Hazrat to miss a single salat and that he would only have to pray Fajr in its earliest time and Zuhr in the end time. The only condition was that he prostrate on a raised pillow for a few days. Hazrat said, "A few days of salat is one too many; I cannot even miss a single *sajda*."

In another incident from *Tadhkirat al-Rashid*:

> He came to Deoband for the annual graduation ceremony. It was likely Asr salat; Maulana Muhammad Ya'qub Nanautawi[60] moved forward to lead the salat. In his haste to catch the *jama'at* (congregational salat), he (i.e. Maulana Rashid Ahmad Gangohi) missed the *takbir tahrima*[61] and reached the imam only a second after recitation had started due to the rush of people clambering to shake hands with him and meet him. After completion of salat, he was somber, his head hung low. Then he spoke [almost inaudibly], "After 22 years, this is the first time I missed takbir tahrima."

Maulana Qasim Nanautawi

It is narrated in *Sawanih Qasmi* that Maulana Qasim Nanautawi fell sick on the return trip from his last hajj. He could not even muster the strength to sit or stand and was constantly retching. The attendant sat him up and he vomited in the receptacle but only bile came out. Then the attendant washed his mouth and lay him back down. A few minutes went by and he sat up retching again. Never did he get a moment in the night or day to sleep in peace. But when salat time came, the vomiting and retching stopped and he prayed without any interruptions. The minute he completed his salat, his vomiting bouts started up again.

Maulana Qasim Nanautawi's wife says,

> His habit was to drink milk before retiring to bed. When he returned after 'Isha and came up (to his room) on the second story, I arrived at his room with the glass of milk. By habit, I knew he was in a good mood if he waited on me and that he was unhappy if he started prayers without waiting. Sometimes, Hazrat spent the whole night in prayer and I would be standing the whole night with the glass of milk in my hand.

Qari Tayyib[62] writes, "Most likely, his intention was to train her in *mujahada* (spiritual struggle) [to increase her ranks and closeness to Allah]." Thus he observes, "My grandmother's (Maulana Qasim Nanautawi's wife) habit was to put all her work aside when the *mu'adhdhin*[63] called out *hayy 'ala al-sala* (come to salat), as if she had nothing to do with the world. She completely disengaged herself from everything."

Also in *Sawanih Qasmi*, "His attachment to Allah was so great that he always prayed jama'a with the first takbir and started preparing for salat the minute the adhan was called."

Maulana Khalil Ahmad Saharanpuri

In *Tadhkirat al-Khalil,* the biography of Maulana Khalil Ahmad Saharanpuri, it is narrated that he attended the jama'a, even while he was out on a journey and tried his best to pray on the station platform when the train made a brief stopover (even at the risk of the train taking off without him). In such situations, he preferred Maulvi Zakariyya to lead the salat since he (Maulvi Zakariyya) preferred short salat and recitation. If Maulana Khalil could not pray on the platform for any reason, he would make sure he prayed in congregation while facing the qibla on the train. Even en route to Madina Munawwara, he always alighted his camel and prayed in congregation, which he was very particular about. Even the hardiest of young men got scared of alighting the sometimes irritable camels, but Maulana always dismounted at the desirable time. By the time he performed wudu and prayed with congregation, his camel had passed him far behind. He would run ahead far enough to pray his *Sunna mu'akkada* (emphasized Sunna), then made another run for his camel, grabbed onto the saddle straps, and mounted his ride. When the time for the next salat came near, he dismounted and walked until the time for salat came in. Then he completed his salat with jama'a and mounted his camel again. Although he walked many miles by doing this, he never tired or gave up and would say, "One can understand the importance of *qasr*[64] here. If you have to run so much for two rak'a, imagine how much you would have to run for four."

Maulvi 'Abdullah Jan (a famous solicitor from Saharanpur) writes:

> I have noted a special quality in Hazrat that always left a strong impression on me. Whenever he prayed, I observed him in a state of complete humility, calm and absorbed, as stated in the hadith [*worship Allah*] as *if you see Him* (Bukhari). I am grateful to Allah that since

my childhood, my upbringing, learning, and sitting have always been with scholars, but I cannot find a more beautiful example of anyone who prayed like he did. I have seen everyone itch in salat, but Hazrat looked as if he was oblivious of any need. In fact, even when he had a cold or cough, I never saw him cough during salat. Though, I did notice numerous times how as soon as his salat ended, he broke out coughing. He would stand up, come by the gutter, cough up phlegm, and clear his system. Then, when he started salat again, it was as if he never was sick. I always thought that this is what is meant by *hudur qalb* (presence of the heart). When I first realized this state, I started observing Hazrat closer and continued observing him from close quarters for many years. I never saw him pray in a sitting position in sickness except on one occasion when two attendants propped him up so that he could pray Maghrib, as per his request. At that time, he was so sick that there seemed no hope of recovery.

Maulana Zafar Ahmad 'Uthmani[65] narrates,

I remained in his service for six years but cannot recall a single time he missed the first takbir of salat. However, one morning, while he was performing wudu, his gums started bleeding; as much as he tried, he could not stop the bleeding. He sent an attendant to the masjid to tell them not to delay the jama'a because of him and said, "I cannot stop the bleeding from my gums." On that day, he missed the takbir tahrima but not the rak'a. For the past six years, I have had the honor of being in the company of Hazrat on numerous occasions at home and on the road, but I never saw him skip tahajjud.

Shaykh ul Hind

After tarawih, Shaykh ul Hind's Ramadan routine was to listen to Qur'an the whole night. The reciters changed [every hour or so], but Hazrat remained standing until his feet started swelling up. He would be so happy when his feet swelled up because he saw himself as a reviver of another Sunna: *hatta tawarramat qadamahu* (until the Prophet's feet swelled; Bukhari).

In *Hayat Shaykh al-Hind*, Hazrat Mian sahib writes of Shaykh ul Hind's routine in Malta,

> During his confinement in Malta, Hazrat was reserved and quiet and perpetually engrossed in the remembrance of Allah. Sometimes, he made dhikr or tasbih; after 'Isha, he read his daily devotions for a short period and then lay down to rest. He awoke again in the extreme cold and performed wudu with freezing water. He moved about quietly to avoid awaking or disturbing the sleep of others and performed tahajjud in the room designated for tahajjud prayer. After tahajjud, he returned to his room and sitting on his charpoy, engrossed himself in meditation and silent dhikr until dawn. After Fajr salat, he remained seated on the prayer mat in meditation. After sunrise, he prayed *Ishraq* and returned to his room for a cup of tea. Then,

he recited and translated the Qur'an or taught Maulvi Wahid Ahmad.[66] After the midday meal, he lay down for *qaylula* (afternoon nap) and then after wudu, recited Qur'an and the du'a booklet *Hizb al-A'zam*. After Zuhr, he either sat to teach Maulvi Wahid Ahmad or translated the Qur'an. Sometimes, he took a walk to the other camps to meet friends. After Asr, he remained quietly engrossed in his daily devotions until Maghrib using his tasbih, which was usually tucked away under his shawl. Near Maghrib time, he ate with friends (attendants), then returned to his quarters and again engrossed himself in the dhikr of Allah. He followed the same routine after Maghrib, engrossing himself in dhikr and nawafil until 'Isha.

In the harsh winters of Malta, he had no choice but to make wudu with freezing water in the open fields, but it never brought any change to his daily routine. During his confinement, he became withdrawn and disapproved of meeting, associating, or keeping company with anyone. He met, but only out of need. In Maulana Hussayn Ahmad Madani's words, "Sometimes, it seemed like he was averse to talk to us."

Upon his return to India, Hazrat once confided in Maulana Asghar Hussayn, "What a great thing this single-mindedness is! I often wished [the quality of my confinement was] enhanced by the absence of my friends (attendants)." The blessed month of Ramadan started on his return journey home [to India]. Fearing he would arrive too tired to complete the Qur'an in India, Maulana Hussayn Ahmad Madani led him in tarawih in which he completed one whole Qur'an.

CHAPTER FOUR

Zakat

Maulana Ilyas Kandhelawi

To the best of my knowledge, zakat never became obligatory on anyone of my Elders of Deoband, at least, in their earlier years. Two stories are well-known about my uncle (Maulana Ilyas), which have even appeared in various publications. Once, he sent a letter from Nizamuddin (near Delhi) to me, "I have wanted to write you a letter for many days, but did not have the funds, and I did not feel right about taking a loan for the sake of a letter. Today, I received some funds and am sending a postcard." In those days, sending a postcard cost only two paisa.

The second story told about him is the famous *gular* story.[67] I am not a witness to this incident, but it was shared with me by my relative who was the imam of a masjid in Delhi. These were Hazrat's first years [i.e. the work of tabligh had not yet started]. He (my relative) thought Hazrat was the shaykh of Delhi and thus must receive delicious foods in Ramadan.[68]

He arrived in Nizamuddin (where Hazrat stayed) at Asr time. It was Hazrat's routine to chant dhikr loudly from Asr to Maghrib. At *iftar*,[69] he would ask the attendants if there was anything to eat. If anything was available, they presented it to him and that would be his iftar and dinner (i.e. he did not have a light iftar and then a full meal later). Anyhow, when the time of iftar came, and Hazrat asked the usual, "Is there anything?"

The helpers replied, "Hazrat, nothing but the gular from yesterday."

My uncle was ecstatic. He said, "Great, perfect! Bring it."

My half-hearted relative, who also joined Hazrat, ate four to five gular, drank a little water, and thanked Allah. My uncle's habit was to eat before Maghrib jama'a and then after Maghrib, stood up to recite Qur'an in nawafil until 'Isha. About ten to twelve minutes before the adhan of 'Isha, he made the salam [i.e. completed his nawafil] and lay down in the masjid. The attendants massaged his feet and then [he rested] until a few minutes before the congregation stood. Then, he made his wudu and came forward to lead 'Isha. He always led tarawih himself and recited at a calm pace; he completed it in an hour and a half.

Meanwhile, my relative went inside and ate in the house. In the meantime, my uncle fell asleep almost immediately after tarawih and often said, "I fall asleep so fast I don't even recall putting my head on the pillow."

My shaykh (Maulana Khalil Ahmad Saharanpuri) and my father had this unique ability to regulate their sleep; they could fall asleep whenever they wanted and wake up whatever time they chose to wake up.

In those days, my uncle would sleep and wake up at about midnight, which was his routine throughout the year. He attended to his washroom and made wudu while an attendant boiled an egg or two for him. Then he stood up and prayed until ten to twelve minutes before dawn. After salam, he asked the attendants, "Anything for *suhur*?[70]" They said, "The gulars from last night." He ate four or five and took a few sips of water. My poor relative, seeing this, decided it was time to take leave for Delhi. He came to Hazrat after Fajr and asked to leave, but my uncle laughed [knowing why he wished to leave] and refused. He explained that he needed to tend to some work and run many errands, but Hazrat refused and said, "Not today." My relative thought, "What was I thinking when I came here?"

The second day after Asr, Hazrat, according to his daily routine, was busy in loud dhikr while my relative was dreading the sight of gular for iftar again. Shortly before Maghrib, a big pot of chicken biryani from Delhi was carried into the khanqah; suddenly, the whole masjid was filled with its spicy aroma. My uncle said in iftar, "Come Brother Latif! This biryani came especially for you; for us is the gular."

Maulana Hussayn Ahmad Madani

If Shaykh ul Islam (Maulana Hussayn Ahmad Madani) ever happened to travel from Deoband to Peshawar or Calcutta, he would say (and this happened on multiple occasions), "I only purchased the ticket up to Saharanpur because I don't have the funds to go any further." Then, I would loan him money so he could continue on his journey. Sometimes, I literally had nothing to loan him, but then my whole life ran on loans. I quickly borrowed from someone and passed the money on to him. When he received his fortunes,[71] he dispatched a messenger with a money order and fees to repay me. When he stopped over on his return trip, I argued with him (as was my usual habit): "Why purchase a money order and pay homage to the *Farangi* (Englishman)?[72] Wouldn't this fall under the definition of *mawalat*?[73] You could have paid me in person upon your return!"

Hazrat's response was always the same: "Death could come at any time."

I quipped, "Why, yes, of course, I would have grabbed you by the collar on the Day of Judgment (demanding that you pay my loan), wouldn't I have?"

The general opinion was that Maulana Hussayn Ahmad only borrowed from Shaykh ul Hadith because no one else would loan him money in Deoband. That may have been a credible reason except for the fact that Hazrat knew me since I was twelve and thus felt most comfortable borrowing from me. But, this is not the time get into this topic.

There are so many anecdotes about the harsh conditions Maulana Hussayn Ahmad faced soon after migrating to Madina Munawwara that I don't even know where to begin. But if anyone would like [to read the full details], they can be found in *Naqsh Hayat*.[74]

Maulana Yahya Kandhelawi

For as long as I can recall, my father always lived in debt (and died in debt). At the time of death, he owed eight thousand rupees, which was incurred neither by overspending nor by necessary expenses, but because of his love for publishing and printing the works of our Elders, which was only greater than my own [love for the Elders]. The large-scale dissemination of the *Bahishti Zewar*[75] was in no small part the blessings of Hakim ul umma, Maulana Ashraf 'Ali Thanawi, the practicality of the book, and then my father's commitment to distribution of the *Bahishti Zewar*.

His printing press was churning out *Bahishti Zewar* almost incessantly throughout the year. Every time a volume sold out, he sent out an order for five thousand more copies [every out-of-stock volume was reprinted in sets of five thousand]. Each copy sold for about 7 ½ paisa, excepting the *Bahishti Gohar* volume. The wholesale price for booksellers was seven paisa, and my father would say that he who did not buy at least ten complete sets was not a true bookseller. This is why many people pooled their funds to purchase ten complete sets of *Bahishti Zewar* and *Bahishti Gohar,* which retailed for 2 ½ rupees. They sold each set at 2 or 2 ¼ rupees which collected enough profit for them to pay for one whole set of their own.

My father visited his shaykh Maulana Rashid Ahmad Gangohi often. If he found out that anyone at the khanqah was in need of help, he would give him five-six sets to sell, told him to keep such-and-such amount and send the remainder to him.[76]

After my father's death, I received letters for many years from customers who wrote, "Your father sent many copies of *Bahishti Zewar,* but I forgot to pay for them. Now, here I am sending the payment," or, "I did not pay then, but now I have no money. Please, would you forgive me and write off the debt."

Another of my father's habits was to never keep money on his person. He would immediately send anything to his creditors, except for the pocket change, which he gave to us. He always said, "If I die during the night, I would not like death to come upon me while I have any money on my person." There are many similar incidents of this kind among my Elders.

Haji Imdadullah Muhajir Makki

It is narrated in the biography of the Leader of the Group, Haji Imdadullah[77] in *Ap Biti*.

We have heard many stories of Haji Imdadullah and the hard times that came upon him. Hazrat Maulana Ashraf 'Ali Thanawi writes, "After his shaykh Mianji Nur Muhammad passed away in 1259/1843, his heart was overwhelmed by love for Allah. That day, he dropped everything, walked out of the village and into the woods. Despising the company of all creation, he wandered in the jungles of Punjab and spent most of his time on an empty stomach, as was the Sunna of the Prophet ﷺ. Sometimes eight or nine days would go by without as much as a morsel going down his throat. But the empty stomach and pangs of hunger revealed many spiritual secrets to him.

He would relate, "One day, I was so weak from the pang of hunger, I requested a small loan to alleviate my condition from a friend who expressed the sincerest friendship for me. I knew he had the money, but he bluntly refused. My heart was tormented and I felt a sorrowful change come over me by this most fortuitous of circumstances. After a few short minutes, an epiphanic state overcame me, and I saw that this incident was brought on by the True Doer of all actions. Then my sincerity reached new heights and my heartbreak converted into joy."

Maybe this is one incident and the Makkan one another because Hazrat Hakim ul Umma narrates an incident that was shared by Haji Imdadullah,

> When I arrived in Makka, I was struck by hunger and had nothing to eat for many, many days. I said to my Lord, "Lord, this tribulation

is beyond my strength to bear." Then I saw Khawaja Mu'inuddin Chishti[78] saying, "Allah will place lakhs of rupees at your disposal." I replied, "I do not have the strength to bear this." He laughed and said, "Your need will not cease (i.e. your reliance on Allah will remain strong)." From that point, my minimum monthly stipend never fell under 100 rupees. Allah grants from His abounding treasures.

Hazrat Shaykh ul Islam writes, "I myself have heard the Pole of the Worlds, Haji sahib, say, 'For one week, I had nothing to survive on except the water of Zamzam. Meanwhile, I asked a sincere friend, who was most outstanding in his claims of love and sincere friendship for me, for a small loan, but he claimed to be penniless, though he was not, and refused. I realized that his refusal was the divine will at work. So, I also was quiet and did not react." There are many other such anecdotes, but it is not to our benefit to compile them all in this letter.

Maulana Rashid Ahmad Gangohi

It is written about Hazrat, the Pole of Guidance, Rashid Ahmad Gangohi:

During his years as a student in Delhi, he never troubled anyone about his meals. His maternal uncle sent him an allowance of three rupees every month. After it ran out, if it had to be, he would suffice on stale bread, lentils, and vegetables, or whatever else came his way. This allowance also sought to cover his other necessities of laundry and stationery supplies. He occasioned to meet an alchemist in Delhi who noted his noble conduct and wished to impart the ancient formulae of alchemy to him, but his austere nature recoiled from even the thought of it."

I once heard my father[79] say, "Once I was teaching Tirmidhi and the chit[80] turned up between the pages in my book. One of the people said, 'Make me a copy of the chit.' I just handed him the original. What was I going to do with it?"

In another place (in the same book), Maulana Rashid Ahmad Gangohi is quoted, "My family and I suffered hunger, but by the grace of Allah, we never borrowed from anyone."

It is written in *Tadhkirat ul Rashid* that the emir of Afghanistan, Habibullah Khan (1872-1919), sent his emissary with five thousand rupees for Hazrat with the message, "You will receive this amount annually and the only condition is du'a."

But Hazrat returned the amount. The emissary begged, "At least respond to him with a letter acknowledging my meeting with you, otherwise, he may think I pocketed the money." Hazrat wrote a letter in Persian:

> I am your brother in Islam, and my heart always supplicates for you, and even more so after hearing about your love for Islam and your patronage of the sacred knowledge. May Allah grant you with many blessings. I received your gift, but now that I have reached an old age and Allah has granted me a lot, what am I going to do amassing so much wealth? This is why I am returning it. You may invest it on other equally noble causes, and regardless, consider me one who is devoted to supplication for you.

Maulana Qasim Nanautawi

I have also heard innumerable stories of the ascetic ways and the hunger of Maulana Qasim Nanautawi.

Hazrat never held in his possession a cloth bundle, a trunk, or even a box;[81] there was nothing to be had in the room of this Recluse of the World. Yes, he did possess a broken charpoy, which it seems, he had devoted the rest of his life to.

No special preparations were made before a journey. If he owned an extra pair of clothes, it was left for safekeeping with someone, but his journey was mostly covered with one pair. However, he did carry a blue lungi with him wherever he went. If his clothes became grimy, he removed them, wrapped his lungi, and put his clothes to be laundered, which he washed himself.

After this, Shaykh ul Hind asked, "What pair of clothes? Without a kurta,[82] he wore an achkan[83] or *angrakha*[84] and pajamas. In cold days, he wrapped a short *imama*, but usually donned a Sherpa hat throughout the winter. In the last illness from which he never recovered, the following was his garb: a grubby, torn imama with several creases; as it was cold, he also donned a thick, blue, patched-up undershirt without any kurta or angrakha over it. A thick, blue blanket hemmed with intricate design and partially ripped and fading, and in some parts, completely faded, was wrapped over him.

Maulana Ahmad Hasan Amrohi narrates his personal account:

> [It was monsoon season and] A small creek [had] flooded over onto the road from Shahjahanpur to the *Khudashanasi Mela*.[85]

Maulana, who was on foot, treaded into the creek, soaking his pajamas. Once he crossed, he removed the pajamas and wrapped the lungi. He rinsed the pajamas, hung it over his staff like the ways of the villagers, and continued on his way.

Hazrat Maulana Muhammad Ya'qub writes:

After my father (Maulana Mamluk al-'Aliyy) passed away, I was going to my house that was located in the Chailonwali neighborhood of Delhi. Maulvi sahib (Maulana Qasim Nanautawi) came to meet me. On the terrace was a large broken charpoy, which was his preferred sitting place. Sometimes, he would order chapatti and nibble on that for many days. I had a servant who baked and served the chapatti. He was given specific orders to serve Maulvi sahib curry with the chapatti whenever Maulvi sahib ordered it (i.e. curry). But he never did except on occasion, and even that after much insistence. Most of the time he was happy with a few pieces of stale bread.

Maulana Amiruddin narrates:

Once, a telegram came with an offer for a high-paying teaching position for 500 rupees a month. I said, "Qasim, you must go!" He replied, "They make me a high offer only because they think I am learned. The problem is that I know I am not." I insisted he (i.e. Maulana Qasim) accept the offer, but he turned it down.

It is written in *Arwahe Thalatha* that Nawab Mahmud 'Ali Khan always desired to meet Maulvi sahib (Maulana

Qasim), but Maulvi sahib avoided him as much as Nawab Mahmud 'Ali Khan desired to meet him. Therefore, he came on two occasions to meet Maulana in Meerat and two times in Aligarh, however, when Maulana found out, he sneaked out of the city and said, "Deliver two of my messages to Nawab sahib: one, to build a masjid at the Ghaziabad Railway Station (G.R.S)." His second message was most inexplicable: "If he does (i.e. build a masjid at the G.R.S), I will carry one side of his palanquin."[86] Nawab sahib was amused upon hearing the second message and as for the first, he said, "I have already sought permission, but have been refused."

The story of his marriage is most interesting, as narrated in *Sawanih Qasmi* by his wife. She said:

> When my father, Shaykh Karamat Hussayn, the overlord of Deoband, married me to him, he sent me off with a generous dowry of precious gems and filigreed jewelry, ornate dresses and outfits, and sets of brass cookware, as was customary in that time. When he came to me on the first night, he started with nafl salat. After completing his salat, he came to me and said most earnestly, "Allah has brought us together, so we must live in harmony; but, under the present circumstances, that may be difficult as you are well-to-do and I am a poor man. Under these circumstances, only two options are available to us: either I raise myself to your level in wealth or you lower yourself to mine in poorness. My acquiring riches is a difficult proposition and that leaves us with only one option, which is that you join me. He spoke some more in the same vein. At the end,

he said, 'if I ask of you something that is to your own benefit, will you put your trust in me?'

He repeated this many times and then finally I said, "I put my trust in you.'

He said, 'remove all your jewelry and allow me full right over your clothes and cookware.'

She said, putting all her trust in him, 'I surrender everything to you.'

The next morning, he piled up all the jewelry, clothes, cookware, and utensils, which were worth thousands of rupees, and gave it all in charity to the Sultani fund."[87] She further adds, "When I came home, my stately father saw my neck, hands, and feet bare of any ornament and asked, "Where is your jewelry?" She went on to narrate the proceedings of that first night. Shaykh Karamat Hussayn said nothing more, but ordered many sets of jewelry. He was worried that it did not befit the poor [newly-wedded bride] child to visit her relatives bare of jewelry. Maulana's wife says, "I returned to my in-laws once again bejeweled. Hazrat came at night and again broached the topic of the Hereafter and again asked for me to forego my right over the valuable collection of wealth to him. But, as I had already done that, what question could there be now of revoking that right. As before, he was told, "You have full right over all my things." Again, the next morning, he gave everything in charity to the Sultani fund." Hazrat's wife frequently said, "After this, all my love for wealth, rupees, and jewelry was forever zapped from my heart. In fact, I started feeling an aversion to the material of this world. Thereafter, I never bought any jewelry, nor did I desire to wear any expensive gowns and dresses throughout my life."

Maulana al-Hajj Qari Muhammad Tayyib reports, "Once, one of Hazrat's admirers gave an expensive shawl and gold jewelry to give to his wife. Hazrat passed on the trust to her, but also reminded her of his right in the following words, "The heart is certainly most delighted with the shawl and jewelry, however, they both will soon lose their lustrousness after a few days of use." Additionally, he said, "A cotton shawl can fulfill the same purpose as the silk one. In return, Allah will reward you with a most durable attire and everlasting jewelry." Thereafter, the wife heartily surrendered both gifts to him.

Maulana Ilyas Kandhelawi

While in Gangoh, my father also pawned some of my mother's jewelry to pay for the expenses of printing *Bahishti Zewar* with a conceited *sahibzada*[88] who thought himself wise beyond his years. He had melted the jewelry and converted it into a nugget. My father was shocked and asked what he had done. He coolly replied, "The value of gold has gone up." My father said nothing more, but my mother replied, "I doubt I will make any jewelry out of it; my days for these things are gone. Now you may use this to pay your debt."

I would like to share another story that somewhat relates to the above topic. In 1374/1955, my daughters and I went for hajj. I asked them to turn their jewelry over to me. [I said], "Whoever falls short (in paying the necessary hajj expenses), I will pay the difference." They all happily surrendered their jewelry to me. Maulana Hussayn Ahmad Madani accompanied us on this journey along with Maulvi Yusuf[89] and Maulvi In'am[90]. This anecdote is mentioned in detail in *Ap Biti.*

Maulana Khalil Ahmad Saharanpuri

Maulana Latif ul Rahman says of Maulana Khalil Ahmad Saharanpuri, as stated in *Ap Biti* (v.6), "I came with a bowl to Hazrat's private quarters. Hazrat's attendant, Haji Maqbul, walked in. I complained that the lentils from the madrasa kitchen were inedible and said, "Please pass me some curry." He replied, "There is none today." I said, "Then give me from Hazrat's curry." He said, "There is no curry even in their house; they are in a state of *faqa*[91] today." I then said, "Oh! Then I will go to the bazaar and grab something for him." Before I knew it, he was at my feet, pleading, "I ask you, in the name of Allah, to never do any such thing for I will be scolded for exposing a secret of the house." Whenever Hazrat came out of his house, he put on the most comeliest garment so that no one would know the better that they were in faqa.

When Maulana Khalil Ahmad Saharanpuri joined Mazahir ul 'Ulum, Saharanpur[92] in 1314/1897 as a teacher, he rented an apartment that was adjacent to the madrasa for two rupees per month. This remained his residence until he migrated to Madina Munawwara in 1344/1924. It consisted of an outdoor kitchen located under the overhang of a small hut. Opposite this hut was a shanty covered by a thatched roof. The shanty was where Hazrat spent most of his time. The roof often caved in [to the elements] every four to five years, only to be replaced by a new one. People insisted he install the more durable tin roof, but he would say, "But why? How long are we to live anyway?" When the roof leaked, which even I saw dripping on many occasions, he would simply shift his belongings to another part of the room. But, he never budged from his opinion that a tin roof should not be installed.

When any female guests came, he would relocate to the madrasa. Special guests like Maulana Rashid Ahmad Gangohi's daughter, Safiyya, would stay for several days (she most often stayed for two days at his place and the remaining few in this worthless one's (i.e. Shaykh ul Hadith). During that time, Hazrat slept in the madrasa to avoid forcing her to cover herself every time she passed by the shanty to attend to her toiletries.

But, once he migrated to Madina Munawwara in 1344/1926, the whole apartment was remodeled with the small room and shanty leveled and converted into a verandah.

Even the bathroom roof left much to be desired, which barely covered more than the toilet area itself. I have yet to understand how Hazrat lived there. However, the humble dwellings of my Elders were no different. If it was owned, the dwelling was plain and small, and if a rental property, the rent was a trifle sum.

Then the successors came and suddenly the homes became larger and grander. I saw their lives (i.e. of the predecessors) personify the transience of the *dunya* (temporal world). Maulana Rashid Ahmad Gangohi's house had a small room that was later converted into a storage space for his belongings. It was always kept under lock and key, and the keys remained with him alone. Hazrat carried his food outside into the courtyard or in the verandah, but that small room always remained for his personal use only.

Maulana 'Abdul Rahim Raipuri

The earlier years of Maulana 'Abdul Rahim Raipuri saw much hunger and hardship. Better days came in his last years but that too punctuated by hard times.

Once, Mulla 'Abdul 'Aziz came and said, "The wood and grain stock has dwindled and we have nothing to purchase more with." Hazrat didn't say a word then, but he (i.e. Hazrat) says, "On that occasion, I invoked Allah in the heart and said, "O Generous one, this is Your creation engrossed in recitation of Your book and Your sacred knowledge. Are they to go hungry? Then it hit me that I should mind my own business, so I invoked, 'if You wish to keep us in this state, then grant us patience, as this is only in Your hands.'" Night came. The grain storage was depleted and the last of the wood stockpile had been used, but Hazrat was neither anxious nor worried. It never even occurred to him to ask for a loan. Some of the boys who bathed in the large stream early in the morning came running and said, "Hazrat ji, wood limbs are floating on the water." Hazrat's face beamed with joy and he said, "The Generous one has sent your sustenance to you. Go and collect as many as you can." The students went running back. They dammed one part of the stream and collected as much wood as they could. In two hours, they had gathered so much they could hardly stack any more. Maulana 'Ashiq 'Ali's commented on this anecdote: In monsoon season, the rains raised the rivers' water levels so high that the limbs, twigs, and boughs were carried off in the current. As for wood, it was for the taking, which is why the students collected and carried them away.[93]

And now, for the matter of the empty grain storage. Two hours later, the mailman came and delivered a money order [in Hazrat's name] for the amount of 150 rupees [a large sum in those days] with a note, 'I send this for the madrasa of Qur'an. Please put it to use for that purpose.' Hazrat asked the name of the donor, but could not recall anyone one by the given name. He stated, "I said to him (the mailman), more than once, that it must be a mistake for I do not even know this person, but he insisted, 'the money order bears your address and your name, whether you know the person or not; there is no doubt that it is meant for you.'" Hazrat finally accepted the money order and handed it to Mulla 'Abdul 'Aziz and said, "Here, now, Mulla ji! Allah has provided for the grain and firewood of His guests. As it is now time for dinner, quickly order the flour; we already have the firewood. Cook thick, thick chapattis; they can be eaten with salt."

There are numerous incidents of this kind from Hazrat's life. In the latter years, Allah provided in abundance; though, Hazrat disliked ownership and possession over anything. At noon time, he said, "Bhai, see what someone has slipped under my pillow," and then it was distributed among relatives and the needy. At the end of his life, he even gave the little clothes he owned to his special attendant, Maulana 'Abdul Qadir Raipuri[94] and said, "Now I will borrow your clothes for the remaining days of my life," though Maulana 'Abdul Qadir never wore them out of respect for his shaykh.

Maulana 'Abdul Qadir was in charge of the Jum'ua sermon in the khanqah[95] and only possessed a single pair of clothes, which he washed and then wore for Jum'ua. One day [the clothes took time to dry and thus], he arrived late for Jum'ua. Hazrat grilled him about why he was so late, but he was quiet. He finally said (that he only possessed a single pair). Hazrat scolded him, "What are these clothes for, to cast in the fire?"

The point is that Maulana 'Abdul Rahim Raipuri was of the persuasion that he must own nothing.

Maulana 'Abdul Qadir Raipuri

It is written that when Maulana 'Abdul Qadir Raipuri [still a fresh graduate from the madrasa] first arrived in Raipur (to his shaykh's khanqah), he received one roti daily, and even that was one-half dry, half-baked, and the other half fully baked but without any curry. Sometimes, he washed it down with buttermilk, but only when someone gifted it from any of the nearby villages, otherwise, he washed it down with water. He narrates, "The brothers from Uttar Pradesh (U.P.)[96] would portion out their roti, one half for the day and the other for the night; I, the Punjabi,[97] would eat the whole roti all in one go and the other time was only *Allah, Allah*." He relieved his hunger by scouring for edible plants and bushes in the nearby jungle, subsisting on a variety of different ones. He heated up the hardened molasses he found in the kitchen until it became syrupy and mixed it with the tea grounds he collected from the bottom of the guests' tea cups and ate it with his roti. At the dump, he found an old quilt, trashed by its owner. Hazrat scavenged and washed it and then double folded it and laid it out near the shanty where Hafiz Yusuf 'Ali tied his horse. That was to be his bedding and *musalla* (prayer mat) for the next 14 years.

There was only one lantern in the khanqah and scorpions, centipedes, and snakes infested the khanqah from the nearby jungle. Hazrat says, "I kept a broken bamboo stick near the bed and sometimes struck it against the ground to scare the scorpions and snakes away."

There are many stories of Hazrat in his biography. Another story: he says, "It was winter time with no blanket or duvet to keep me warm. In the evening, I sat from Maghrib to 'Isha near the place where the wudu water was warmed and completed my litanies there. After 'Isha, I closed the doors of the masjid and rolled up in the straw mats. But my head remained exposed to the chilly air. I stayed rolled up in the mats for some time and then unrolled myself and started the dhikr. I spent the whole night keeping myself warm with the chant of the dhikr. The winter season passed by in this manner, but I never complained of my situation to anyone nor did anyone find out." He also said, "The first winter passed in this manner, but hereafter, I received a new blanket every winter."

All the Elders showered this lowly one with affection and love, but unfortunately, I still never changed for the better. Anyhow, if he ever received high-quality blankets, Maulana Abdul Qadir Raipuri would mail it to me straight away. But, this lowly one, who never got into the habit of wearing nice, new clothes as it already had been squashed under my father's shoes[98]—I have already narrated this in *Ap Biti*—would carefully wrap the comforter in a canvas and then save it for my daughters' bridal gift whenever they got married. All of my daughters' bridal comforters came from Hazrat. He often gave them to me when I came to visit him, and if I ever insisted he gift it to his attendants and helpers, he would say, "Do not refuse when I give to you; I give it by order." And then I could say no more.

Maulana Hussayn Ahmad Madani' (2)

The first years of my Elders' lives were difficult. Shaykh Maulana Hussayn Ahmad Madani writes of the first few years of his life in Madina Munawwara in his autobiography, *Naqsh Hayat.* Conversely, his last years were prosperous. As mentioned earlier, the emir of Kabul sent 5,000 rupees for Maulana Rashid Ahmad Gangohi, but he refused the gift and returned it. It is also narrated in the biography of Hakim ul Umma, Maulana Ashraf 'Ali Thanawi, that money orders were frequently returned to their senders. It is narrated in the biography of Maulana Qasim Nanautawi that once he was getting a haircut in the Chaththa Masjid when Nawab 'Abdul Karim, the nawab of Meerat, came specially to visit him in Deoband. Maulana had already seen him from afar. When he came close, shaykh affected aloofness and turned away as if he had never seen him. The nawab folded his hands respectfully, a big wad of notes rolled up in a handkerchief in his hand. He remained standing for some time. Finally, shaykh turned around and said, "Ah, Shaykh sahib! Hope you are well?" Nawab sahib greeted Maulana with salam, kissed his feet, and laid the rolled up wad of notes at his feet. The shaykh nudged it away with his foot. Then, the Nawab held his palms together in deference to the shaykh and pleaded with him to accept the gift but Maulana Qasim refused. The Nawab finally stuffed the notes in the shaykh's shoes. When he stood up, shaykh casually shook the shoes and the notes drifted to the ground. The shaykh wore his shoes, chuckled, and said to Hafiz Anwar ul Haqq, "Hafiz ji, we earn money and so do the lovers of dunya; the difference is that we renounce it and it falls at our feet, while the lovers of dunya fall at the feet of dunya and it spurns them." Saying this, he distributed the notes among those around him.

Beside one or two, I do not know of any of the Elders who kept money on their person. If any needy person came, they secretly helped them out and no one knew the better. I did personally experience a common episode with Maulana Hussayn Madani on many of my trips with him. Sometimes, when it got hot, shaykh would hang up his achkan and lie down for a short nap. Someone would come along, rummage through the pockets, and take whatever they fancied to gain his 'blessings'. Sometimes, the shaykh would know that so-and-so came and emptied out his pockets. He then took a loan to pay for his train ticket and refused to disclose the name of the thief who filched him.

How can I ever do justice to their beautiful conduct? There are thousands of such anecdotes filled with their awe-inspiring traits and habits. I just wish I, and others of my ilk, could be blessed with even an iota of their beautiful character.

CHAPTER FIVE
Fasting and Ramadan

Maulana Ilyas Kandhelawi

As far as fasting and nawafil are concerned, we know little about the routine of our Elders since they tried their best to conceal that aspect of their lives. My uncle's (i.e. Maulana Ilyas Kandhelawi) time in Gangoh was a period of intense hardship. Since the hakim forbade him, he never drank water for seven years. In extreme thirst, he either washed out his mouth with water or took a fruit. I accompanied him on many occasions to an invitation and knew his predicament. I would be sitting next to him. He carefully prepared the morsel and even feigned chewing and eating it, but the morsel eventually went in my mouth. He would keep his fast and no one would even know.

Maulana Hussayn Ahmad Madani

I have already dictated two anecdotes about Shaykh ul Islam Maulana Hussayn Madani. The first was that he was very particular about fasting on the first days of Dhul Hijja, even when he was traveling, and said to me, "Make sure to fill the thermos with chai,"[99] but my wife never took any of that. She woke up early, prepared the tea, boiled some eggs, and since I rarely slept in those days, he took his suhur while I did my own work. After he departed for the train station, I would go to bed. At suhur, my wife signaled me with a cough and I brought the suhur for shaykh. But, he got angry and said, "Why do you put your wife through difficulty?" I would say, "I never woke her up. She gets up on her own out of her zeal [to serve the Elders]." When I said, "However, I never will come in the way of any good deed,"[100] the shaykh would laugh.

The second anecdote is from 1326/1908, which I also dictated earlier. Shaykh secluded himself for a few months in the khanqah of Gangoh. During that time, I stood outside my house before sunset every single day. My mother prepared the iftar and laid it out on the charpoy. I remained standing by the door and the minute I caught sight of him coming, cried out, "He is coming, He is coming!" And I made myself a guest to his iftar meal. Shaykh also mentions this incident in many of his correspondences and writings saying, "I know him since he was eleven years old." Since then, his love and affection for me only increased.

Maulana Rashid Ahmad Gangohi

The way he and the Elders anticipated fasting in the month of Ramadan was unequalled. Two gatherings were held daily in Maulana Rashid Ahmad Gangohi's place for eleven months: the morning gathering after 9 a.m. for a select group,[101] and the second, from Asr to Maghrib for the public. But on the 29th of Sha'ban [a day or two before Ramadan], he shook hands with everyone and said, "Now is recess time for one month. What could be more regretful than a person wasting his time in the blessed month."

I have narrated many incidents in my book *The Ramadan of the Elders*. I will reproduce some here to serve as an example [of how they devoted themselves to the blessed month].

It is written that Maulana Rashid Ahmad Gangohi worked himself so hard in his devotions in Ramadan that people would have pity on him. When he was well over 70 years old, he was fasting the whole day, praying between six to twenty nawafil after Maghrib in which he recited at least two juz, and prolonged his ruku' and sajda so much that an observer would think he is suffering from amnesia. After salat, he recited several juz during his walk home for iftar, the period he was in the house, and then on his return for tarawih to the masjid. Then, he attended 'Isha and tarawih, which took approximately an hour or hour and a half. He fell asleep at about 10-10:30 p.m. and woke up at about 2-2:30 a.m. Some of his attendants even found him performing ablution at 1 a.m. on a few occasions. Then he prayed tahajjud for two and a half to three hours. Sometimes, an attendant came to remind him of suhur and found him engrossed in prayer at 5 a.m. After Fajr, he was busy in his *aurad* (loud litanies) and *muraqaba* (meditation) until 8-8:30 a.m. Then he prayed Ishraq and rested for a short time before the mail arrived. After checking and responding to the mail, he dictated fatwas, prayed his *duha* (pre-noon salat), and then made qaylula. After Zuhr, the doors of his chambers were closed and he recited Qur'an until Asr. He suffered severe sciatica in the aforementioned Ramadan and was forced to stop to rest on his way to the bathroom, although it was only fourteen to fifteen steps away from his chamber, but still, he never prayed his nawafil in a sitting position. When the attendants pressed him to pray tarawih sitting down, he refused and said, "This is a sign of being fainthearted."

Maulana Qasim Nanautawi

I never learned of the routine of Maulana Qasim Nanautawi except that it is known that he memorized the whole Qur'an on his maritime journey to Hijaz in the Ramadan of 1277/1861. He memorized one juz each day and recited it in tarawih that very night. However, [according to another report] he himself says that he memorized the whole Qur'an in two Ramadan.

After he completed memorization, he devoted much of his time to recitation. Once, he recited 27 juz in one rak'a. [To reconcile the report that he memorized the whole Qur'an in one Ramadan and his own account that he did it in two] it is most likely he memorized a quarter juz every day in the first Ramadan and then completed the remaining in the second.

Haji Imdadullah Muhajir Makki

Regarding the routine of the Leader of the Clique, Haji Imdadullah Muhajir Makki, Maulana Ashraf 'Ali Thanawi writes that Haji sahib said to us, "I say this for your own good that this fakir never slept on most nights of his youth, especially the nights of Ramadan. After Maghrib, two youth, one Hafiz Yusuf, son of Hafiz Zamin,[102] and the second my nephew, Hafiz Ahmad Hussayn, led me in salat. They recited one juz and a quarter each until 'Isha.

After 'Isha, two fresh huffaz would lead and then another hafiz until midnight, and then another two in tahajjud. In summary, the whole night was passed in this manner."

Maulana Khalil Ahmad Saharanpuri

An incident is narrated about Maulana Khalil Ahmad Saharanpuri in *Ap Biti* that he was extremely sick in one Ramadan with dysentery. It was hot and searing winds were blowing across the region. For many days, he broke his fast with medicine and never consumed anything. Jum'ua came and Maulvi 'Abdullah Jan, the solicitor, came to pray Jum'ua. He saw his pallid face and frail body and could not hold himself back. He hid behind one of the pillars and started to cry. Maulana 'Abdul Latif asked, "Hazrat, you have not eaten for days and are suffering. It would be good if Hazrat makes up the fast at a later time. After all, the *fuqaha* have given dispensation in this matter, and then, Maulvi 'Abdullah is over there crying." Hazrat was startled and he said, "What are you saying, Hafiz sahib? Fast, and that the fast of Ramadan?" Then he said, "When Allah is the Changer of hearts then how is it that a self-possessed man like Maulvi 'Abdullah Jan loses his composure."

It is written in *The Ramadan of the Elders* that Maulana Khalil Ahmad Saharanpuri led tarawih himself, and since he had memorized at an older age and was in a state of spiritual absorption during recitation, he occasionally stumbled in recitation, though he rarely ever made mistakes. People traveled from afar to pray behind him; some completed their own tarawih earlier to join him. He would say, "I make ruku' but feel as if I will not be able to get up for the next rak'a. I complete twenty rak'a thinking in each rak'a that I am going to fall; and rising from sajda is harder than climbing a steep mountain."

After Fajr, he remained engrossed in his litanies until early morning. Then he sat down for research on his *Badhl*[103] until 11 a.m. Thereafter, he went home and rested for a short time. After Zuhr, he recited Qur'an to Hafiz Muhammad Hussayn who came especially for this purpose from Ajrara. He usually recited tasbih from Asr to Maghrib and rehearsed Qur'an twice with my father. After Maghrib, he recited the juz of tarawih in his nawafil and then came home, sat with the family, and then rested for a short while. In Madina Munawwara, he had assigned Zakariyya[104] to wake him up at eight Arab time.[105] But whenever I went, I found Hazrat performing his wudu. After *Badhl* was completed, he used that time for recitation of Qur'an and to study Wafa' al-Wafa.'[106]

Shaykh ul Hind

Regarding Shaykh ul Hind Maulana Mahmud al-Hasan, I mentioned earlier that he passed the whole night listening to the recitation of Qur'an. The huffaz[107] alternated, but he remained standing throughout the night.

Maulana 'Abdul Rahim Raipuri

Before the partition between Pakistan and India [in 1947], over 500 people came to spend Ramadan with Maulana 'Abdul Rahim Raipuri,[108] but no one was allowed to talk or meet with him [throughout the month]. The closest they got was when he appeared from his private chamber to go to the masjid. Everyone would then stand up in their spots to get a glimpse of him. However, his special attendants like Maulana 'Abdul Qadir Raipuri and Maulana Allah Bakhsh were allowed to sit and maybe get a word or two with him during the brief interval in which Hazrat drank two or three cups of tea after tarawih. Only one time, he suddenly raised the topic of *Haqiqat e Muhammadiyya*[109] and expounded it for over 2 ½ hours for many days consecutively. There is truly no end to how much we can delve into the lives of our Elders.

Maulana Hussayn Ahmad Madani

I have narrated the daily routine of Maulana Hussayn Ahmad Madani for the month of Ramadan in detail in *The Ramadan of the Elders*. I was very blunt. So once, he [i.e. Shaykh ul Hadith][110] passed the comment that Hazrat (i.e. Maulana Hussayn Ahmad Madani) is so obsessed with Congress[111] though Haji Imdadullah, Maulana Rashid Ahmad Gangohi, and Shaykh ul Hind have entrusted you with some work[112]—I have narrated the whole incident in detail somewhere—Hazrat did not say a word and listened attentively. When I had finished my rant, he still had not lost any of his cool. He looked to me and said, "I am not ignorant of what you say. This is why I spend my Ramadan in Silhat (Bangladesh) because the people of U.P. have no mind to do anything. I spend my Ramadan there (i.e. in Bangladesh) in peace. I receive no newspapers and hear no political discussions."—I have narrated the whole incident in detail in *The Ramadan of the Elders*—Thereafter, it became his habit to save the letters he received from his disciples regarding their spiritual exercises, devotions, and dhikr in his travel bag and present it to me whenever he came to Saharanpur. Handing them to me once, he said,

"Here, read these." I was stunned. Some of them had a daily routine of 125,000 times of dhikr daily and likewise other exhaustive devotions.

Maulana 'Abdul Qadir Raipuri

Hadrat Maulana 'Abdul Qadir remained ill until the end of his life, but even then, maintained silence in his private chamber. I have mentioned one incident like this in *The Ramadan of the Elders.* According to my routine, I recited one juz after Zuhr and took off for Bahit House (residence where Maulana 'Abdul Qadir was temporarily residing for treatment). Altaf bhai (one of shaykh's personal attendants) had allocated a small area in the private chamber for me. I would enter there quietly and warned the attendants not to inform the shaykh of my arrival. One day, I came as usual and sat in my retreat as shaykh took his medicine. After Asr, I saw and was dazzled by an effulgence of light like I had never seen before. I wondered that if this is the state of some people's iftar, one can only imagine what their fast must be like.[113]

I have dedicated a separate book to the Ramadan of the Elders. Whoever wishes to learn more, may read *The Ramadan of the Elders.*

CHAPTER SIX
Hajj

Maulana Hussayn Ahmad Madani

I have already quoted Maulana Hussayn Ahmad Madani about what he said when he came [to meet Shaykh ul Hadith] on the 9th of Dhul Hijja. I knew he was fasting so there was no question of eating and drinking. I offered him a bottle of *'itar* to put on. Suddenly, a sad look came over him and he said, "Today, the lovers [i.e. the hajis] are forbidden from applying fragrance." Then he took the bottle and put some on.

Maulana Rashid Ahmad Gangohi

In a time of dire need, Maulana Rashid Ahmad Gangohi was overcome by a sudden urge to go to Hijaz. He had not a penny on him, but Allah fulfilled his wish. The story is that Deputy 'Abdul Haqq Rampuri was going for hajj and sponsored a large group to accompany him. It crossed his mind to take Hakim Ziya'uddin and Maulana Rashid Ahmad Gangohi—the story is long and narrated in full in *Tadhkirat ul Rashid*— as well. Maulana Abul Nasr[114] sold everything he had in his house and took his wife along for the journey [so he could be with shaykh]. One cannot compare the journey of our time to those. First, they traveled on [backbreaking] bullock-drawn carts to the port and then rode the waves on sailing ships (*baghlas*) for months in extreme danger [seasickness] and toil. The voyage took many months, and then, they had to board cargo vessels that anchored at every port to load cargo. The transit took anywhere—the details of the hardship are narrated in detail in *Tadhkirat ul Rashid*— from three to four months from Mumbai to Jeddah. Hadrat made this voyage in 1280/1863-64. Coincidentally, a fierce storm swept the seas that very year, but Hadrat was a model of equanimity.

His second voyage was in 1294/1877 during the Russo-Ottoman war (1877-78). Other scholars learned of his plan and decided to accompany him on the voyage though, rumor had spread that he is going to enlist against the Russians under the pretext of hajj. The following elect scholars joined Hadrat:

1. Maulana Qasim Nanautawi
2. Maulana Muhammad Mazhar
3. Maulana Muhammad Ya'qub
4. Maulana Rafi'uddin
5. Shaykh ul Hind Maulana Mahmud Hassan

Altogether, over a 100 scholars accompanied him on this [epic] voyage. Though direct train and ship routes to Jeddah were open, they were forced to transit many times to arrive at Jeddah. During the journey, Maulana Ya'qub and Maulana Qasim held lively discussions on clairvoyance and unprophetic miracles (*karamat*) while Maulana Rashid Ahmad Gangohi was quiet and only listened. Most people considered the first two saints, while Maulana Rashid

Ahmad merely a Maulvi, though he was a top jurist and a *faqih ul nafs*.[115] Once they both said of Maulana Rashid Ahmad [countering the general perception that he was just a Maulvi], "What do you say of Rashid Ahmad; he has absorbed everything [all the highest spiritual states] but never lets anything out. We are small vessels that can barely contain anything within ourselves."

He was as scrupulous about salat on journey as he was about it at home. Usually, Maulana Rashid Ahmad or Maulana Ya'qub led the salat.

Many karamat took place on this voyage, but I will only narrate one. It was time for Fajr. Maulana Rashid Ahmad came off the train, performed wudu, prayed his Sunna, and led the salat. When the train conductor blew the whistle, many of the congregants quickly broke their salat and hopped on the train. Hadrat, in the meantime, continued praying. Only after he completed the salat, made his du'a, and boarded the train, did it start moving [from the platform].

Many similar incidents have taken place with my Elders. How many times the whistle blew repeatedly [signaling departure time], but strangely enough, the train never moved [until they boarded].

They stayed in Mumbai for 22 days as the ship had not yet arrived at port. One day, Maulana Ya'qub announced that since some of Maulana Nanautawi's companions have yet to join them, the ship will neither arrive nor depart. And that is exactly how it transpired. The ship reached port the very day the said companions arrived, and by happenstance, Haji Qasim opened the ticket counter on that very day.[116] Many other similar incidents took place, which are mentioned in *Tadhkirat ul Rashid*.

Shaykh's third and last hajj was in 1399/1882. People

refused to purchase tickets since few days remained for hajj (fourteen days to be exact). They said, "With only fourteen days left, ten of which will be in quarantine at the port of Kamran, there is no point in going.[117] Hadrat still purchased the tickets and said, "We will definitely make it for hajj." Many people stayed behind while others purchased tickets and arrived at Jeddah port. Though local authorities did their best to bar entry, the ship still somehow docked and unloaded its passengers onto the holy land. On the return journey, the ship was forced to quarantine for twenty days instead of the required ten days at the port of Kamran, but [that was of no concern since] Hadrat had gotten his hajj.

Maulana Qasim Nanautawi

Maulana Qasim Nanautawi performed three hajj. The first hajj was during his days in hiding.[118] Maulana Ya'qub Nanautawi says,

> When Haji Imdadullah fled, I thought to myself, 'I should also accompany him.' Maulana Qasim had already received permission from his parents to go. Aside from the few provisions I had, I was nearly penniless, but Maulvi sahib (Maulana Qasim Nanautawi) provided for my needs until I was able to arrive safely. Maulana himself was cash-strapped, but for his complete reliance on Allah, he also reached safely without any issues. In Jamadi ul Thani (6), 1277/1860, we took boats and paddled through the rivers of Punjab to Sindh; then we snuck our way to Karachi where we boarded a ship [for the holy land] and arrived in Makka Mukarrama

at the end of Dhul Qaʻda (11). After hajj, we departed for Madina Munawwara and returned to Makka Mukarrama in the beginning of Safar (2) [1861]. We boarded a ship at the end of the same month [of Safar], reached Mumbai in Rabiʻ ul Awwal (3), and arrived home in Jamadi ul Thani (7).

Once again, he was preparing for hajj in 1285/1868. And there, yet again, he took off with a few people. Then, in 1294/1877, Maulana Rashid Ahmad Gangohi made plans for hajj. I got ready and convinced Maulana Qasim to join us. All of his devotees and attendants who accompanied him departed in Shawwal (8), 1294/1877 and returned in Rabiʻ ul Awwal (3), 1295/1878. The whole caravan comprised of scholars with some eighteen to twenty Maulvi Fadil.[119] The whole voyage went smoothly. After meeting Haji Imdadullah and visiting many of the holy sites, Maulana Qasim suddenly fell sick in Jeddah. The painful separation from his shaykh (Haji Imdadullah), the sacred sites, and then the continuous walking became the scapegoats [for his sickness], but truth be told—he was ailing even before hajj. We boarded immediately upon reaching Jeddah as we had heard that the ship was ready to leave port and that the next ship was scheduled to arrive in ten days; in fact, two weeks. So, we decided to [board this ship and] reach Mumbai in fifteen days and face whatever unpleasant situations that come our way. And truly, it just so happened that we faced as many hardships going as we did ease and comfort coming. Two days after boarding, Maulana was racked by fits of coughing and a fever. The ship offered no comfort; additionally, nothing was at hand to calm him nor any medication to prescribe, and nothing to be done to alleviate the issue. The illness went from bad to worse, and then, one day, he fell so sick that we all thought that his end was near. To add to our troubles, some type of epidemic broke out on the ship taking one or two lives daily. We finally arrived in the Port of Aden (Yemen) and the ship was, as expected, quarantined. Locals were barred from boarding and passengers were banned from disembarking. Then the ship ploughed on to Mukalla (also Yemen and to the east of Aden) where it anchored for a short time. Lemon was purchased from the hawkers while we came across watermelon, rose, and some medication in the ship itself. The doctor onboard gave him quinine and advised him to eat chicken. But, where were we to find chicken? [The same doctor came to the rescue and] kindly gave from his own provisions. The fits had weakened him and he still could not stand the sight of food, but his desire to eat indicated that he was in recovery. When we reached Mumbai, he could barely keep himself in a sitting position. After three or four days, we set out from Mumbai for home. Though it was winter, hot winds in the Jabalpur area made Maulana's condition worse. By the grace of Allah, we had lemon, coconut, and other such edibles in our possession, which he ate, but he was also given water. Soon after reaching home, he fully recovered and regained his strength, though the cough stuck on, and he also occasionally suffered asthma attacks. Although it became more difficult for him to talk for long stretches of time, his condition did improve in general. Then in Sha'ban (8) of the same year, we received news from Rurki that Pundit Niyanand was in town harassing and provoking Muslims by raising objections against Islam. The Muslim community pressed the Maulana to come, which he did despite his terminal illness and fragile condition.

Shaykh ul Hind

Shaykh ul Hind performed two hajj, the first of them in the company of the great shuyukh in 1294/1877 (the spiritual liveliness of this hajj was beyond any description). They were greeted at every station by a large crowd. Shaykh ul Hind received authorization of hadith from Shah 'Abdul Ghani on this very journey.[120] He stayed in Makka Mukarrama for one month, and on the request of Maulana Qasim Nanautawi, Haji Imdadullah took him in bay'a and then granted him khilafat immediately thereafter.

Shaykh ul Hind served Maulana Qasim Nanautawi with all he had during his illness in hajj. On the return journey from Mumbai, he dropped his blessed teacher off at Nanauta before he went on to Deoband.

He also had planned a hajj with Maulana Ahmad and Maulana Habib ul Rahman in 1308H/1891, but [his shaykh] Maulana Rashid Ahmad Gangohi refused him permission.

His second and final hajj was the historic and famous hajj of 1333/1915, which has been reviewed in numerous periodicals and magazines. He met with Jamal and Anwar Pasha [two high-level officers in the C.U.P (Committee for Union and Progress)[121]] but was eventually arrested by the British. All plans, hopes, and dreams came to an end by a simple stroke of destiny. Though Maulana Khalil Ahmad Saharanpuri was not on the same ship with Shaykh ul Hind, he performed hajj in that same year. Later, Shaykh ul Hind was arrested and exiled to the island of Malta. I have mentioned earlier that my Elders' early years were marked by adversities and tribulations. But in the end, Allah showered them with countless blessings and they were helped in unforseen ways, as is well known.

With some of the Elders, all these blessings went in the way of handouts and sadaqa [to different people]. Maybe it has been mentioned earlier that Shah 'Abdul Rahim was overwhelmed by such bounties. When he wished to rest at noon or at night, people slipped money by his head instead of giving it to him directly. Annoyed, he said, "Bhai, look at what is by the pillow," and when the attendant would inform him that it is such-and-such amount of money, he said, "Go and give some to so-and-so and this-and-that much to so-and-so." The same affair played out in the night, and again, the monetary gifts were distributed among attendants, relatives, and guests.

Maulana Khalil Ahmad Saharanpuri

My shaykh (Maulana Khalil Ahmad Saharanpuri) never let an opportunity to go for hajj. A small monetary gift was quickly given in charity but the larger amounts would be saved for the next hajj. He performed seven hajj.

His first hajj was in 1293/1876. At the time, he had just taken up a teaching position in Bhopal. He had no funds to make hajj but was eager as ever to go. His agreement with the madrasa stipulated that any teacher granted leave for hajj would receive advanced salary for the months in which he did not teach. The dean though did not honor the agreement and gave only a meager sum. Never mind that, Hadrat arrived in (his hometown) Anbehta [to join the caravan of relatives that were going for hajj], but it was too late as they had already departed. He was alone and had never been for hajj before. Fear of the unexpected and the long and dangerous journey was unnerving, yet he put his matters in the hands of Allah and decided to go. After receiving permission from his parents and shaykh, he departed by himself, entrusting his two year son and three month old daughter to Allah. Upon reaching Mumbai, he found out that his relatives had already boarded the first ship, so he purchased a ticket for the next one. Once, narrating the story of this first hajj, he said, "The minute I boarded the ship, I started feeling nauseous and was taken by vertigo. I vomited for the next three days and had no desire to eat anything. When I felt a little better on the fourth day, I got hungry. I poured lentils in a pot, which I put up on the [portable] stove to make *khichri*.[122] Prior to this, I had never cooked anything in my life. I checked and saw the water was boiling. The lentils had cooked, but the rice still needed more time. I added salt [to make it cook faster] but ended up putting so much that I could barely put it to my tongue. I resigned myself to my fate and stored my pot away. One of the nawab from Bhopal area was also going for hajj. I was 24 years old at the time and at the peak of my youth. He happened to pass by, saw me, and asked, "Who is with you son?"

I responded immediately, "Allah."

He did not say anything more, but after reaching his seat, he sent for me. He had prepared dinner for me and said, "Son, from now on, you will eat with me."

I said, "I feel ashamed of joining you without compensating you, but if there is any way I can be of service, I will not hesitate in the least to take you up on your offer." The nawab paused for a moment and then asked, "Do you know how to write?"

I replied, "I do."

Saying that, I jotted something down and passed it to him. He was impressed with my writing and handed me a manuscript he had brought along with him. He asked me to copy it in neat handwriting. I assigned myself a certain number of pages every day and joined him for dinner daily. This saved me from loneliness, but also from preparing food. A few days later, when the port of Jeddah came into view, I said to him, "The porters are heavy-handed and will throw the luggage around so I suggest you leave this part of the job to me." My first job was to gather all the baggage and advise all the nawab's servants to stand around and not let anyone come close to it. I had included the few belongings I had in the heap. I could speak Arabic fluently so the minute the ship docked and the horde of porters jumped aboard, I pulled one aside and cut a deal with him to carry all the baggage for a specified amount. I showed him the heap and told the servants who were still standing guard to count the baggage and allow the porter to take it away, but reminded them to be vigilant of anyone else trying to touch it. First, the baggage was carefully loaded on to the boat and then we boarded. The nawab praised my management and the way I oversaw the whole operation. He had noticed the chaos that broke out and the frustration of the hajis as they disembarked. There were numerous complaints of lost baggage and scenes of sulking hajis all over. Once we entered the city, I handed the original manuscript and my handwritten copy to the nawab and sought his permission to be on my way. The nawab was unhappy and said, "Under no circumstances can I let you go until we return home." I told him that I have not come to work or secure a job and explained that if I come to the house of Allah and still remain a servant of His creation, then what is the purpose of coming so far. "Now that I have reached the door [i.e. we are close to Makka Mukarrama], there is absolutely no way I can accept your offer."

Anyhow, I separated from the nawab, mounted my camel, and rode off. I already had a home and a place to stay in Makka Mukarrama as Haji Imdadullah was there. I came straight to Hazrat and enjoyed homemade food day and night. I spent all my time in the company of Hazrat, in the Haram, and remained busy in tawaf and salat.

After hajj, I decided to go to Madina Munawwara, but everyone warned me that the journey was unsafe and dangerous. Haji Imdadullah asked, "So what is your plan Maulvi Khalil Ahmad? I have heard the route is treacherous and many of the hajis are turning back home." I said, "I have decided to go to Madina Munawwara because death is destined and cannot be changed. If it comes en route, then what better way to die? I have come this far by the mercy of Allah. Now, if I abandon my trip out of fear of death, then who could be more unfortunate than me." Hearing this, Hadrat's face became radiant and he said, "That's enough, that's enough; my opinion is also that you go, and you will reach, by the will of Allah." I met Hazrat and departed for Madina Munawwara, and only my heart knows with what peace of mind and heart I reached Madina Munawwara. I stayed there for two weeks and then returned home to meet my shaykh."

The following year, Maulana Khalil Ahmad Saharanpuri wished to join the caravan of scholars going for hajj, but Maulana Rashid Ahmad Gangohi forbade him.

He performed his second hajj in 1297/1880. The story behind it is that Maulvi Shamsuddin, a judge in Bahawalpur, wished to take Hadrat, who tutored Maulvi Shamsuddiin's children and stayed at his residence, for hajj. He already had a strong liking and a lot of respect for Hadrat, but would also have the advantage of being accompanied by a pious, knowledgeable, and experienced scholar to guide him through the rituals of hajj. Hadrat, in the meantime, heard that Maulana Rashid Ahmad Gangohi and Maulana Ya'qub are planning on hajj again this year. Hadrat was already upset over not being able to accompany his shaykh on the previous hajj (1877) and took Maulvi Shamsuddin's offer to accompany him for hajj as a Godsend. He wrote a long letter to his shaykh expressing his eagerness to go for hajj. He elaborated upon his situation and then asked for his shaykh's decision on the matter. In reply, Maulana Rashid Ahmad Gangohi granted him permission and advised him to take along extra provisions in case of an emergency so that he would not be dependent on others. Maulana Rashid Ahmad Gangohi further explained that sometimes the *kafil* (guarantor) assigned to the haji dies or a disgruntled kafil sometimes may abandon the haji due to a difference in temperament. In such cases, the situation can turn ugly. To avoid such potential obstacles, Islam permits taking precautions, however, whatever is destined will happen regardless. In the letter, Maulana Rashid Ahmad Gangohi also noted, "Now, listen to the servant's state (i.e. Maulana Rashid Gangohi). The heart desires to do good (i.e. to go for hajj), but the body is weak and provisions are scant. This is why nothing can be said (of whether I will go or not). If the strength builds up and fate prepares for all the necessary provisions, then who knows, otherwise, the intention is not firm. The rumor [of my going for hajj] is false."

When shaykh arrived in Makka Mukarrama, Maulana Rashid Ahmad Gangohi wrote to his shaykh, Haji Imdadullah, requesting him to grant Maulana Khalil Ahmad Saharanpuri with khilafat. Haji Imdadullah was pleased with Hazrat's spiritual progress and in Muharram (1) of 1297H/1880, granted him khilafat and stamped [the authorization certificate]. He took off his own imama with elation and placed it on my shaykh's (i.e. Maulana Khalil Ahmad Saharanpuri's) head. My shaykh placed both of these honors at the feet of his shaykh (Maulana Rashid Ahmad Gangohi) and said, "I am unworthy of these. These are the blessings of my shaykh." Shaykh replied, "Felicitations to you," and then, signing the authorization certificate of khilafat, presented it with the imama to Maulana Khalil Ahmad Saharanpuri. This same imama my shaykh gave to my father saying, "Until now, I was the guardian of this imama, which you are most worthy of. By returning it to its rightful owner, I have released myself of my duty and authorize you [as follows]: if any seeker turns to you, accept him in bay'a and teach him the name of the Most High."

The third hajj was performed in 1323H/1905. His wife and daughter accompanied him on this hajj. The wife financed her trip by selling the land she had inherited from her previous husband, while the daughter did so by selling her jewelry. After completing his hajj, Shaykh stayed in Madina Munawwara for 23 days and then departed at the end of Shawwal (10) for home. The shaykh performed this hajj to help ease the loss of his shaykh, Maulana Rashid

Ahmad Gangohi [who passed away the same year].

In the hajj of 1328/1910, shaykh came to Delhi to say farewell to Hadrat Shah 'Abdul Rahim Raipuri who was going for hajj. Shah Zahid Hassan insisted upon shaykh to go for hajj and said that he (Shah Zahid Hassan) will go if the shaykh goes. Shaykh (made the decision then and there to go and) departed for hajj with Shah Zahid Hassan, but not before dropping his wife at home and assigning his lectures on hadith to Maulana Yahya Kandhelawi [at Mazahir ul 'Ulum, Saharanpur]. My father never accepted a salary for substituting for his shaykh, though he did collect the shaykh's salary on his behalf (for the duration he substituted for the shaykh) and sent it to *Amma ji* (lit. mother; i.e. Shaykh Maulana Khalil Ahmad Saharanpuri's wife).

He arrived at Makka Mukarrama on the 6th of Dhul Hijja (12), (and after completing his hajj) reached Madina Munawwara via Rabigh on the 10th of Muharram (1). He remained in the blessed city for the next 22 days and then arrived in Saharanpur in the last part of Safar (2).

The fifth hajj was with Shaykh ul Hind in 1333/1915, though they did not travel on the same ship. He departed in mid-Shawwal (10) and arrived in Makka Mukarrama on the 22th of Dhul Qa'da (11). After hajj, he came to Madina Munawwara on the 7th of Muharram and returned to Saharanpur nine months later in Shawwal (10), 1334/1916.

His sixth hajj was in 1338H/1920. He departed in Sha'ban (8) and like every other journey he made to the Arabian Peninsula, the rumor had spread that he is migrating to Madina Munawwara. Zakariyya also accompanied shaykh on this journey. Shaykh wanted to stay longer in Madina Munawwara, but soon after arriving in Makka Mukarrama, he met Maulana Muhibuddin, a clairvoyant and khalifa of Haji Imdadullah. He was close friends with the shaykh and received him with a hug. He said, "Where have you come? [Don't you know that] The disaster is approaching?"[123] Maulana Muhibuddin insisted he return back home immediately, but shaykh said, "There are many in my group who are performing their first hajj, and now that I am here, how can I leave before completing my hajj?"

The Arabian Peninsula was in upheaval when the shaykh sent us off to Madina Munawwara in Shawwal (8). The main routes were unsafe, so we took [the southern] alternate route through Mount Gha'ir, the same route which is said to be taken by the blessed Prophet ﷺ in the Hijra. No pilgrim was allowed to stay longer than three days in Madina Munawwara unless he could convince his bedouin guide and pay him a guinea a day. By the mercy of Allah, it so happened that one of the camels from our caravan died on the way. The camel owner insisted he be paid his daily charge—shaykh had already paid for our journey and stay in Madina Munawwara—but when he did so, we got on his case about our lack of provisions. And then one of us filed a complaint with the local authorities that we only possessed funds for a three-day stay, and so they (i.e. the authorities) petitioned for the pilgrims with the guide. In this way, we were able to stay for a month in Madina Munawwara. It is the strangest and most unusual circumstance that came upon us.

After hajj, we departed at the end of Muharram (1) and arrived in Saharanpur in Safar (2).

Shaykh never returned to the Subcontinent following his seventh hajj in 1344/1926. His devotees from Hyderabad had extracted a promise from him to visit and stay in Hyderabad for a week en route to hajj. So, shaykh and Zakariyya arrived at Mumbai[124] from Hyderabad while all other companions went directly from Saharanpur to Mumbai. After arrival in Madina Munawwara, shaykh visited Jannat ul Baqi' often, whereas all the other companions returned to the Subcontinent in their own times.[125] In this last hajj, Maulana 'Abdul Qadir also arrived in Madina Munawwara at the end of Sha'ban (8).

This letter has drawn on, but I [cannot finish this letter without] reproducing a letter[126] by Maulana Hussayn Ahmad Madani that is relevant to the topic.[127] He writes:

Respected one!

We owe servitude to Allah because that is what His attributes necessitate for two reasons:

1. He has absolute power to cause all benefit and all harm.
2. He is the Beloved.

The meaning of the first is embodied in the word *jalal* (lit. to be sublime, great, and exalted), while the second in the word *jamal* (lit. beauty). But, these two are not adequate expressions because jalal alone is only an offshoot of the ability to harm (i.e. it is not 'absolute power to cause all benefit and all harm'), while jamal itself is only one of the many *asbab* (means) for being beloved (i.e. jamal is not His belovedness itself but a means to His belovedness). [So, for example,] belovedness of Allah can also be attained through closeness to Him and realizing His kindness and compassion.

The first of the two reasons that necessitates servitude to Allah must be confined to the boundaries of the intellect (and cannot be expressed in words). In this servitude, the servant has a vested cause for worship, which is either hope or desire or both. This is why his servitude cannot be perfect servitude as much as the servitude that is for the pleasure of Allah alone. It is understood that whatever servitude and submission there is to the beloved is to seek the pleasure of the beloved, and this is why it is important to incorporate both types of servitude in the complete faith. The type of worship the first type of servitude to Allah engenders is salat and zakat, while the second, fasting and hajj. Fasting is the first stage of love for the beloved, while hajj the second.

The explanation of the above outline is that the first obligatory upon the fervid lover (*'ashiq*) is to sever relations with all others [beside Allah], which culminates in fasting. If the day is for fasting, then the night is for standing (in *salat al-tarawih*), and whatever relations are withstanding, are severed at the end with the Sunna *i'tikaf.* The ayah, '*So whoever sights [the new moon] of the month, let him fast it* (2:185) and *whoever fasts in Ramadan with faith and expectant of reward, all his past sins will be forgiven'* (Bukhari 1/16) emphasizes the obligation of standing throughout the month.

But, the main components of fasting, which is prohibition from three acts (food, drink, and intercourse), cannot constitute the perfect fast [of a fervid lover] without abstinence from sins and abidance to the base desire. *Whoever does not avoid lying and acting upon it, Allah has no need for his abstinence from food and drink* (Bukhari 3/26), and *how many fasters whose fasting is only hunger and how many worshippers in salat whose standing is nothing more than wakefulness in the night* (Ibn Maja 1/539) are clear proof of this. When the first stage of severance of all others is accomplished (which is the first valley of fervid love to be traversed), we must move on to the second stage, which is the abode of the beloved and fawning oneself at His place. This is why the days of hajj succeed the days of fasting, which culminates with the Day of Sacrifice on the tenth. The voyage of the fervid lover who has severed all ties with all others and who is a claimant of true, fervid love will not be in an ordinary way. He is oblivious of the state of his head and his feet, unmindful of his look and dress, nor does he know anything of dispute and quarrel with anyone. *There is [to be for him] no sexual relations and no disobedience and no disputing during hajj* (2:197). What does fervid love have anything to do with argument with anyone and what does spiritual disquietude [that evolves from fervid love] have anything to do with carnal desire. He cares not for *kuhl* [in his eyes], nor does he seek after fragrance and oil. He is loath to populated areas and should seek fulfillment in the woods and wild creatures. *But, forbidden to you is game from the land as long as you are in the state of ihram* (5:96). And hunting game, that wasteful pastime, is despised by the fervid lover and disquieted soul. *But, when you come out of ihram then [you may hunt]* (5:2). His night and day is remembrance of the beloved, to embrace His name and to forget oneself altogether; to abandon loved ones, family, relatives, friends, and comfort and ease. Nothing will satisfy; neither sweet dreams nor delicious foods. All desire for tasteful drinks and elegant clothing will fall away.

يُدَارِيْ هَوَاهُ ثُمَّ يُكْتُمُ سِرَّهُ

He tends to his desire, then hides his secret

وَيَخْشَعُ فِي كُلِّ الْأُمُوْرِ وَيَخْضَعُ

And in all matters is humble and submissive

My respected one, [what I have given you] is just a brief sketch of the hajj and umra. Life is not worth living if the heart does not hunger and the bosom does not ache. He is not human whose heart and mind and primary limbs do not contain the yearning and fervid love. Here, the mind is dazed. The more unconscious the mind is, the greater the [spiritual] turbulence and agitation, the closer one is to becoming a consummate human. It is important for any person who steps into this valley to brace himself for any eventuality and to be passionate [about the path you are on]; and to even think of ease, comfort, self-respect, and the self is the worst and most humiliating sin.

O respected Maulana! You take a step in this endless tortuous valley and then gripe about nausea, dizziness, sickness, weakness, pain, respect, and vanity? How sad! Step forward with a firm foot; if you face anything, consider yourself fortunate; if you are harassed, consider it the grace of Allah. Who [do you think] is behind the scenes, pulling those strings?[128] When Layla dashes the glass to the ground, Majnun's[129] swooning breaks into a trance-like dance manifesting his special love for her, and you, here, are backing out and showing reluctance in this matter? *No, never! No, never! I swear by Allah, those who suffer the greatest hardship are the prophets; thereafter, those closest to them, and then those closest to them,* are the words of the beloved Prophet ﷺ. Remember, a man's price is set by his level of determination and zeal to do something:

$$ بِقَدْرِ الْجَدِّ تَكْتَسِبُ الْمَعَالِيْ $$

You will reach elevated stations according to your effort

$$ وَ مَنْ رَامَ العُلَي سَهَرَ اللَّيَالِيْ $$

And whosoever aims high, will spend the night awake

Beside the pleasure of Allah, one should be anxious for and passionate about nothing else. In this delirious gibberish of mine, I wasted much of your time, and for that I apologize, but what can I do? I am a mendicant of the Order of Chisht; their *nisbat* will show through one way or another. If my point is in error, then shred this letter to pieces and take the words of the Hyderabadi elder as an amulet. On the other hand, if you see any glimpse of truth to it, then do show it to Maulana 'Abdul Bari Nadwi[130] and Hakim 'Abdul 'Aliyy sahib. I think it would be best to appoint Syed Amin 'Asim, who was also the mutawwif for Shaykh ul Hind, as your mutawwif. Though he has passed away, his daughters have taken his place and his grandson, Syed 'Aqil Attas, is serving the hajis and does his very best to look after them. His card is included, and if befitting, then also show him this letter.

Many will offer their services to be your mutawwif in Mumbai and Lucknow but past experiences with such people have proven sour. My older brother, Syed Ahmad sahib, and younger brother, Syed Mahmud Ahmad, are in Madina Munawwara. If possible, then also meet them. If you need anything, they will try their utmost to fulfill your needs. Also, Maulana Shafi'uddin Naghinawi, the servant and khalifa of Haji Imdadullah and the classmate of Maulana Rashid Ahmad Gangohi in hadith who is a pure-hearted person, is also in Makka Mukarrama. Take some time out to meet him and send my salams to him. Also, request his du'a for me.

Try not to waste a moment in the two holy sites and do not let your time pass in ignorance while on the journey. The time in Arafat, after noon, is especially an opportune time. Not a second of that precious time should be wasted. Ignore the faults of the pilgrims and especially of the dwellers and officials, and do keep to yourself. Keep this useless and worthless servant in your pious du'a. Who knows, your du'a may be the means of salvation. It would have been best for you to have devoted a few days to dhikr before you departed for the hajj and visited the holy land so that you gain a realization of the inviolability of these two places. But now that you have made the intention, it is important to follow through with it. As much as possible, do not allow ignorance to make its way and remain engrossed in dhikr. By the will of Allah, I will depart here on the fifth of Shawwal (8), and if Allah wills, Wahid will also join you in hajj. I ask Allah to grant you the blessing of a true hajj and visit to the holy land.

Please pass on my Sunna salam to your mother, associates, and friends.

Servant of the Elders,

Hussayn Ahmad

CHAPTER SEVEN

Taqwa

The essence of all the pillars of Islam is taqwa. Numerous ayah of Qur'an and hadith enjoin believers to acquire the taqwa of Allah. Abu Sa'id al-Khudri ؓ says that a man came to the Prophet ﷺ and asked him for advice. The blessed Prophet ﷺ said, "Hold onto taqwa because it is inclusive of all good."[131] In another narration, "I advise you to have taqwa, as it is the root of all things." In another hadith, "Taqwa is obligatory on your outward and inward."

In the Qur'an, Allah says, *the most respected of you to Allah is the one who has the most fear among you* (49:13). In the Hijra, the Prophet ﷺ reached the area of Banu Salim and led Jum'ua there. After the introductory sermon, he said, "I advise you to hold onto taqwa because the best advice any Muslim can give to any Muslim is that he encourages him towards the Hereafter and reminds him to hold onto taqwa. There is no better advice nor is any dhikr greater than that. The taqwa of Allah saves from the wrath of Allah, His punishment, and His displeasure. It illuminates the countenance, invites the pleasure of Allah, and elevates the status."[132]

Likewise, when Abu Bakr ؓ became caliph, he said [in his first sermon] after glorifying Allah, "I have been appointed your emir though I am no better than you, but it is true that the Qur'an and Sunna say that the greatest acuity is taqwa and the greatest stupidity is transgression."

The number of ayah and hadith on this topic are countless, and in this regard, I have found no one group or individual that can vie with my Elders in the matter of taqwa. There are numerous stories from their life, more than I can ever recount. And then that is not even the objective, but whoever composed the [following] poems about my Elders, spoke the truth; I hold these poems dear to my heart and narrate them in every book of mine.

خدا یاد آوے جن کو دیکھ کر وہ نور کے پتلے

To see them is the remembrance of Rabb, those figures of light

نبوت کے یہ وارث ہیں ظل رحمانی

They, who are the inheritors of the prophethood, shade of al-Rahman

یہی ہیں جن کے سونے کو فضیلت ہے عبادت پر

It is they whose sleep is more rewarding than worship

انہیں کے اتقاء پر ناز کرتی مسلمانی

Upon their taqwa, the submission in Islam is proud

انہیں کی شان کو زیبا نبوت کی وراثت ہے

The inheritance of prophethood most suited their status

انہیں کا کام ہے دینی مراسم کی نگہبانی

Guarding the traditions of Islam was their job

رہیں دنیا میں اور دنیا سے بالکل سے بے تعلق ہوں

Living in the world but detached from it

پھریں دریا میں اور ہرگز نہ کپڑوں کو لگے پانی

Wading in the river but never does a drop wet their clothes

Maulana Muzaffar Hussayn

I have narrated numerous incidents in the sixth chapter of *Ap Biti*. The taqwa of Maulana Muzaffar Hussayn was exemplary. During his years as a student, he never ate roti or curry in the city of Delhi because of the *amchur* (dry mango powder) that was used to prepare the curries, since most buyers purchased the mangoes on speculation (i.e. before they actually grew on the trees [which is impermissible in Islam]).

Also, it was known about him that he could never keep down any doubtful food and would immediately vomit. This is why people were scared of inviting him for food to avoid humiliation. His household and relatives were also careful in this matter. Once, he came to his relative, Maulvi Nur ul hasan's house. Maulvi Nur ul hasan sent his son Maulvi Ibrahim to buy some items from the market so as to avoid an incident. Among the dishes was rice pudding. The second he ate the rice pudding, he vomited. Maulvi Nur ul hasan was confused. He investigated and learned that the milk with which the rice pudding was prepared had spilled. So, the son bought some milk from the confectioner's (*halwa'i*) store on credit and carried it in a bowl.

In another similar incident, when Maulvi Nur ul hasan was a *tehsildar* (tax collector) in the district of Nakur, he sent out one of the workers and prepped him beforehand to do exactly as he instructed, otherwise they both would be humiliated. He stuffed the money in his hands and said, "Make sure you buy the items with this money only," and then dispatched him to purchase jalebis and milk. The worker wondered how they would both be humiliated. He went to the confectioner and purchased the milk and jalebis on credit in the name of the tehsildar and pocketed the money Maulvi Nur ul hasan gave to him. The moment Maulana Muzaffar Hussayn put the milk and jalebis in his mouth, a riot broke out. The worker could never imagine he would be taken to task so quickly for bilking the money.

Once, Nawab Qutbuddin, the author of *Mazahir Haqq* (commentary of Miskhat al-Masabih) invited a few notable people, among them, Shah Ishaq Sahib, Maulana Muhammad Ya'qub sahib, and Maulana Muzaffar Hussayn sahib for dinner. Shah Ishaq accepted the invitation, and so too did all the other invitees, except for Maulana Muzaffar Hussayn. This upset Nawab sahib who took up the matter with Shah Ishaq Sahib (who was also Maulana Muzaffar Hussayn's teacher) saying, "I sent an invitation to Maulana Muzaffar Hussayn, but he refused it."

Shah Ishaq Sahib rebuked Maulana Muzaffar Hussayn and said, "Oh, Muzaffar Hussayn! Have you got indigestion from taqwa or what is the matter? Is his food haram?"

Maulana replied, "No, no, it is nothing like that. I would never question the credibility of Nawab sahib."

"So, why did you refuse to accept the invitation?"

He said, "Hazrat, Nawab sahib invited yourself, Maulana Ya'qub, and many others. He will send a palanquin for you, which will only add to his expense. Then, he is after all a son of a nawab, he will spend lavishly on the invitation. Now, I have been informed that he is in debt; and it is understood that the expense of this invitation exceeds his bare necessity. Thus, why does he not use this money to pay off his debt? In such a situation, eating his food will not be without some form of reprehensibility." Shah Ishaq realized his own part in this [form of reprehensibility] and said to Nawab sahib, "Nawab Qutbuddin! Now, I too will not attend your invitation."

Maulana Ashraf 'Ali Thanawi comments on the statement, 'will not be without some form of reprehensibility': "Attending such an invitation would amount to secondary aiding in *matlun*[133] (unnecessary deferment) of payment of a debt. What a fine level of taqwa and such a dignified and yet humble teacher! He started out rebuking him but ended up following his example."

I have also written on Maulana Qasim Nanautawi that he ate something doubtful but came home and vomited it out. I cannot possibly cover all the stories but would like to narrate a few examples if only to illustrate the taqwa of our Elders. I have written on Maulana Rashid Ahmad Gangohi and how he would stand up and pray, even in the last sickness of his life. I have also written on how he refused to have cataract surgery and said, "A few days of salat is too many, I cannot even bear one sajda in this state [i.e. in a sitting position on a chair]."

The story of Maulana Khalil Ahmad Saharanpuri has also been narrated. Even when it was burning hot, he kept fast and broke it at iftar with medicine only, and continued to fast the whole month of Ramadan. When a large monetary gift came to Maulana Rashid Ahmad Gangohi, he returned it to the sender and said, "I no longer hold classes of hadith."[134] Some people even advised Hazrat not to return it and said, "Ask the sender for permission to spend it elsewhere." He replied, "Why should I go around obtaining permission from people?"

I asked my friend Sufi Muhammad Iqbal Madani to

find and collect the stories of the taqwa of my Elders, which he did. May Allah bless him with the best of rewards for that. It has been published under the title *Akabir ka Taqwa.*

Hakim ul Umma, Maulana Ashraf ʿAli Thanawi, wrote, "Once, I wrote something of my personal matters to Hazrat (Maulana Rashid Ahmad Gangohi). In response he said, 'brother! I have not reached those levels even at this point in my life.'"[135] What humility! Then, Maulana Gangohi once took oath by Allah and said, "There is no excellence in me." Some people were confused by this oath because there is no doubt that the shaykh was blessed with great qualities but that would violate his oath [since he swore there was no excellence in him though he knew there was]. In response, Maulana Thanawi explained, "Elders do not see their excellence in any quality since they are always aiming for higher degrees of excellence [in different qualities]. Hazrat negates his excellent qualities on the basis of the higher degrees he is striving to attain."

Maulana Ahmad ʿAli[136]

Hazrat Maulana Ahmad ʿAli, the commentator of Bukhari, lived and taught [hadith in] Calcutta, but when he came to [his hometown of] Saharanpur on breaks, he would teach in Saharanpur also. Once, he came to the madrasa when Madrasa Qadim[137] was under construction. He immediately packed his bags for Calcutta to collect donations for the madrasa. I saw the ledger on which he had done his math of the expenses of the trip. His calculations were precise; he missed nothing, even the cards and envelopes[138] that he purchased on the way. At the end of the ledger, he writes, "I went to so-and-so place to meet a friend; though I was able to collect more than was expected, I hadn't gone with that intention, so please deduct the expense of that trip from the total amount."

Maulana Mazhar Nanautawi[139]

It was the habit of Hazrat Maulana Mazhar, the first dean of Mazahir ul 'Ulum to make a note of the time he started talking to any of his personal guests who came during madrasa hours. Once they left, he would make a note of the time again and jotted down the date and total time spent with the guest on his journal. At the end of the month, he added it all up, and if the total time was less than a day, he let the administration know that he had taken half a day off, and if more, he would let them know a whole day was taken off from the madrasa [accordingly, they deducted pay from his monthly salary]. Though, if someone came seeking a fatwa, he would not note that down.

Maulana Khalil Ahmad Saharanpuri

When Maulana Khalil Ahmad Saharanpuri returned from his one-year stay in Madina Munawwara in 1334H/1915-16, he refused to take a salary and said that he was too weak and frail to fulfill his duties. He explained that while he was absent [in Hijaz], Maulana Yahya Kandehlawi substituted for him and refused any salary for the duration of his teaching in Saharanpur. "He would teach in my place and took my duties as his own, and both of us together did the work of more than a single teacher. But now that he has passed away and I can no longer continue teaching, I excuse myself from accepting any salary."[140] But Maulana 'Abdul

Rahim Raipuri and Maulana Ashraf 'Ali Thanawi both were senior board members of the madrasa. They pressured him to accept the position of administrator and insisted that the staff will work optimally under his guidance. In addition, he can continue teaching without pay if he is up to it and his health allows. Maulana Khalil Ahmad Saharanpuri accepted the offer.

I have never seen for myself but was told by a reliable source that when a guest came to meet him, he would immediately step off the rug. When asked about it, he said, "The madrasa has only laid out the rug for the teacher to teach on. We have no right to make personal use of it."

I never saw Hazrat sit on a madrasa-owned charpoy; he always sat on the three or four charpoys he kept for this purpose in the madrasa. Before the annual convocation, Hazrat and all the other teaching staff devoted the whole day in the madrasa to prepare for the convocation, but none of them ate from the madrasa. They always ordered food from home, and [whenever they got time] they retired to one corner to have their meal.

Maulana 'Inayat 'Ali

On numerous occasions, I saw the principal, Maulana 'Inayat 'Ali, keep two inkstands in his office, one his own and the other the madrasa's. If he wanted to dispatch a message to his family, he wrote it on his own paper and with his own pen. Likewise, Maulana Zuhur ul Haqq, who was in charge of cooking for guests, never taste-tested the food to see if it had enough salt. He called a student or one of the guests.

Maulana Munir Nanautawi

Once, Maulana Munir Nanautawi, the principal of Darul 'Ulum Deoband, went to Delhi to publish the annual report of the madrasa with 250.00 rupees [from the madrasa funds]. Somehow, the money was stolen, but he never let it be known to anyone what had happened. He went home, sold his land, collected the payment and used it to print the annual report. The madrasa board found out some time later. They wrote to Maulana Rashid Ahmad Gangohi about it and asked for his fatwa on the matter. He replied that Maulvi sahib was a trustee and the funds was lost without malicious intent, therefore, he is not liable to repay madrasa for anything. The madrasa then requested Maulana Munir to accept the money and presented him with Maulana Gangohi's fatwa. He skimmed through the fatwa and then said, "Did Miań Rashid Ahmad learn *fiqh* (Islamic law) for me or is it that the rulings of Islam apply only to me? Tell him to put his hand over his heart [i.e. be honest] and ask him what he would have done had he been in the same situation? Take away this fatwa from me now! I will not take a penny."

Maulana 'Abdul Rahim Raipuri

One of Hazrat Shah 'Abdul Rahim's famous and oft-related quotes was, "Nothing scares me as much as administrating over a madrasa. If an employee falls short in his work or brings any harm to a business, he may seek forgiveness from the owner before resigning from the job or even on his deathbed, but the funds of the madrasa are the donations collected from the poor and laborers.

We board members are only trustees and not owners of the funds. Our forgiving anyone for misuse of the funds of the madrasa means nothing since we have no authority to forgive for something that is not even ours. Yes, this much can be said that if we were to overlook a mistake out of some greater benefit for the madrasa, then we can be hopeful that Allah too will pardon our shortcomings [in administration over the madrasa]. Though, if we look the other way out of personal connections [with the abuser], then we are accomplices to the crime. The perpetrator will not be forgiven in any case because it is a matter of *huquq al-'ibad* (rights of others), and the donors are so numerous that there is no way forgiveness can be sought."

Maulana 'Inayat 'Ali

Maulana 'Inayat 'Ali, whom I mentioned earlier, dedicated his life to the madrasa. He took on every job, supervised every project, and sometimes juggled it all at the same time. He was a teacher [at the madrasa] but also issued fatwas, collected donations from the locals, handled all the legal and court-related issues, took on scores of madrasas projects and fulfilled many other needs of the madrasa. Nowadays, you would need four or more people to manage the amount of work he did on his own. In old age, he became so frail that he came to madrasa in a sedan-chair and then stayed the whole day tending to different tasks. If someone brought the lunch from home, he would eat it cold in one corner of the office. Because of his dedication to the madrasa, I petitioned for him to be granted a pension from the madrasa. The first to oppose my proposition was Maulana 'Abdul Latif, the dean of the madrasa. I said to him, in my typically brusque manner, "You will also reach this point one day [i.e. reach old age and be in need of a pension]." He replied, "When it does, I will open up a *pan*[141] shop near the student campus." Hazrat Maulana Ashraf 'Ali Thanawi wrote the following on my proposition, "Pension is not permissible from the current funds, but if you create another for pensions only, then that can be done. Whatever you said about the principal is correct and I am personally aware of it myself. Whatever amount you feel is reasonable can be collected as a separate fund from friends. I will also contribute five rupees a month to the fund." Many anecdotes of this kind related to the *waqf* (endowment) funds are narrated in the *Ap Biti.*

Maulana Ashraf 'Ali Thanawi

There are even many incidents of this sort about Hakim ul Umma, Maulana Ashraf 'Ali Thanawi. It is mentioned in the biography of Hakim ul Umma, *Ashraf ul Sawanih,* that when he performed wudu in the masjid, he poured the remainder of the warm water into the masjid cistern [to save masjid donations].

Hazrat Thanawi says that when Maulana Rashid Ahmad Gangohi lost his sight, I would never sit and join his gatherings without announcing, "Ashraf 'Ali is here." And when I took leave, I said, "Ashraf 'Ali seeks permission to leave." Hazrat Thanawi says, "To sit in a gathering without informing of one's presence is *tashabbuh bil tajassus* (likeness to eavesdropping) and tashabbuh bil tajassus is also a form of eavesdropping. To inform him of my arrival and departure was beneficial in another way: maybe he would like to say something he would hesitate saying in my presence [i.e. by the habit of announcing my presence, he does not feel any reluctance in saying what he wants since he knows when I am or am not present in the gathering]."

Once, Hazrat Thanawi was traveling by train and it was raining hard. He got off at a small, remote station. [For lack of accommodations,] The stationmaster put him up in a storehouse [near the station]. When night came, he ordered one of the workers to light a lantern for Hazrat, though Hazrat himself was reluctant to use it. Suspecting it was owned by the railway company, he did not wish to bring up the matter with the Hindu stationmaster who may not say anything outwardly but would certainly feel that Islam is overstrict.[142] I was facing this predicament and making du'a in my heart, "Oh Allah, please save me in this situation." He had just made the du'a when the stationmaster called out to the worker, "Don't light the railway lantern; take mine instead." Hazrat was ever so grateful to Allah and said that I would never have used the railway lantern; I would have blown it out and passed the night in the dark.

One of Haji Imdadullah's attendants had saved his (Haji Imdadullah's) *tasbih* (or *subha*; rosary) and wished to present it to Hazrat (Maulana Ashraf 'Ali Thanawi). Hazrat asked, "Did you get this in a permissible way?" He replied, "Haji sahib gave it to me himself." Then for further peace of mind he inquired, "At the time of death[143] or before that?" He replied, "Before the sickness that took his life." Only then did Hazrat accept the gift.

Once, Hazrat Thanawi was traveling by train from Kanpur to Saharanpur. He had sugarcane which he wanted the station workers to weigh so he could pay its fees before he boarded the train, but no one was willing to weigh it for him out of respect for him. Even the non-Muslim workers said he need not worry and that the matter [of payment for the sugarcane] is taken care of. "We will let the inspector know [who inspected the receipt to ensure all fees are paid]."

He inquired, "Where will the inspector stay to?"

They replied, "To Ghaziabad."

"What after Ghaziabad?"

They replied, "He will inform the next inspector."

"Then after that?"

"He will take it to Kanpur and that will be your departure point."

Hazrat said, "No, in fact, the journey will not end there. What about the last leg of the journey to the Hereafter. Tell me what will happen then?"

They were dumbfounded and struck by Hazrat's taqwa.

Maulana Hussayn Ahmad Madani

When Maulana Hussayn Ahmad Madani was released from prison in Karachi, a member of the Bengal Council offered him a position and told him, "We will give you 40,000 rupees in cash[144] and tenure as a professor at Dhaka University at 500 rupees per month. Please do accept it, Hazrat."

Hazrat asked, "What must I do?"

The member whispered, "We only want you to cease all political activities and demonstrating [against the British government]."

He replied, "I cannot ever back out from the path Shaykh ul Hind put me on." Hazrat narrated this incident himself and then advised, "Stay steadfast on this path." We should not forget that this offer was presented to him in 1933 when he was out of work. After two months, he came to Silhat and took a position that offered 150 rupees per month.

Maulana Isma'il Sunbuli, who is also Hazrat's khalifa,

says, "Once, Hazrat was traveling on train in a first-class cabin with a wealthy Hindu. The Hindu went to the bathroom but returned immediately. Hazrat understood immediately. A short time later, he got up and entered the filth-smeared bathroom. He saw a few cigarette boxes strewn about and used them to wipe it down. He returned a while later and wondered, 'Why did you return from the bathroom?'"

The Hindu replied, "It is filthy."

Hazrat said, "That is not so. Please, go look."

The Hindu went to the bathroom and was struck by Hazrat's humanity.

Once, I said to Hazrat, "They may not say it out of respect, but many people have a problem with your salary from the madrasa and these non-stop trips."[145] Hazrat yanked out the agreement that was signed between him and Darul 'Ulum Deoband, which he kept on him at all times, folded neatly in the case in which he kept his spectacles. He presented it to me and ordered, "Read it." The agreement, I realized, gave him considerable flexibility [to take as many trips for his political engagements as he liked though it effected the classes and curricular quota], which made even his frequent trips seem less. But, that was a time when Darul 'Ulum Deoband's[146] closing down or staying open rested on his teaching at Darul 'Ulum. It was also a time when pro-Congress or Congress-run[147] organs and newspapers were opposed to Darul 'Ulum Deoband until Hazrat joined the madrasa. On the other end, there were those who alleged that donations to the madrasa had significantly decreased since he joined,[148] though I can personally vouch for the amount of sacrifice Hazrat made in collecting donations for the madrasa. He returned from every trip with large sums of money and also founded the *ghalla* scheme in Darul 'Ulum

Deoband to generate more donations for the madrasa.

Qadi Zuhur ul Hasan Seharwi narrates: I was the main supervisor of the huge convention of 1920 in Sehara, which was attended by many reputed Hindu and Muslim dignitaries. I sent money orders to reimburse them for their second-class bookings,[149] pay of an attendant, and a small honorarium. Maulana Hussayn Ahmad Madani was living in Calcutta at the time and was one of the dignitaries to whom I had sent a money order. The trip from Calcutta to Sehara was about 24 hours on the Mail Train.[150] Maulana came on his own without a helper or servant and as soon as he entered the convention center, asked, "Where is the supervisor's office?"

He came to me and after salam and a handshake, he rested a paper and some money on the desk and retired to his room. I learned from the paper that he came by third-class and spent only seven *ana* on breakfast. No other scholar or dignitary presented such an austere example. On the last day of the convention, the committee agreed to present him [with an honorarium of] a hundred rupees. When I came to give it, he inquired, "Have you lost the paper I gave you?"

I said, "Not only do I have it but it has already been logged in our records."

"Then, did you not read it?"

I said, "I saw it and have saved it in the ledger."

He said, "Then just give me that amount."

I said, "I am giving you what has been proposed by the committee and you should accept that decision."

He asked, "How many committee members are there?"

I replied, "Seven."

He asked, "Does your budget come from public

donations or your personal accounts?"

I replied, "From general donations."

He objected, "Then you have no right to spend in this manner."

I said, "The public has placed their trust in us."

He said, "They have done so with the understanding that you will spend only as necessary. You do not have the authority to squander funds like this."

I argued further but he was firm and said, "I will take no more than this."

Maulana 'Abdul Qadir Raipuri

Large crowds joined Maulana 'Abdul Qadir on his tours to Punjab.[151] Many times it happened that Hazrat dispatched a message that I am the guest of so-and-so and five others will come with me. Everyone else should look for their own lodgings and food.

Dr. Barkat 'Ali [Hazrat's personal physician] had advised Hazrat [for medical reasons] to stay in Mazahir ul 'Ulum madrasa for a few days. Hazrat's stay always increased donations[152] to the madrasa, but he still paid rent for the room he stayed at under the pretext of a donation to the madrasa. Though he was advised against it numerous times, and reminded that his stay in the madrasa is the need of the madrasa and that it benefits from his stay, Maulana 'Abdul Qadir always paid his own rent and even collected rent from his devotees and visitors from Punjab under the pretext of donations, as they too stayed in the madrasa during that time. He also solicited donations from guests from Pakistan for the madrasa. Likewise, his khanqah in Raipur was on land that was *waqf* (endowment) for a madrasa. He would secretly pay the rent for that too under the pretext of donations.

All the incidents I have noted are whatever readily came to mind. If I remembered or could easily find it [in the books], I jotted it down quickly though, they are not even a shred's worth [of their beautiful biographies]. But, the purpose of this letter is that we cannot just pass judgments or object against anyone. Muftis are required to base their fatwa on the evident, but if they learn of the reality of a situation, then there should be no objection against them modifying that fatwa. In fact, they must modify their fatwa.

These are my fathers, bring the likes of them
If you are going to gather the company, O Jarir!

TRANSLATOR'S NOTE
[1] Relief from worldly and spiritual tribulations
[2] *Matan al-'Aqidat al-Tahawiyya*, 1/81
[3] Al-'Aqidat al-Wasitiyya, *Fada'il al-Sahaba wa Maratibuhum*
[4] Al-'Aqida al-Tahawiya, 1/68

CHAPTER ONE

[5] Maulana Rashid Ahmad Gangohi was a muhaddith, a jurist, and one of the fathers of Deoband. He was born in the village of Gangoh 150 miles east of New Delhi in 1244/182, and is a descendant of the sahabi, Abu Ayyub al-Ansari ﷺ. After completing his primary Islamic studies in Gangoh, he moved to Delhi to study under one of the last remaining students of the Waliullahi chain, Shah 'Abdul Ghani. For further studies, he attended the gatherings of many renowned scholars, but remained dissatisfied either due to his incompatibility with the shaykh or their incompetence, which often forced him to find another scholar. His journey ended with the polymath, Maulana Mamluk al-'Aliyy, a lecturer at Delhi college in 1260/1844. Here, he also met his kindred friend and the founder of Darul Uloom Deoband, Maulana Qasim Nanautawi. Together, they revived the Waliullahi legacy, spreading the knowledge of hadith, instituting the inseparability of both Shari'a and Tasawwuf, and reviving the Sunna in the Subcontinent.

After completing his studies, he gave bay'a to Haji Imdadullah and received khilafat seven days later, but remained in the company of his shaykh for the next 40 days. After the death of Maulana Qasim, he became the spiritual head of Darul 'Ulum Deoband and raised it to prominence.

He taught the six books of hadith in Gangoh where students came from around the Subcontinent. Two of his outstanding works are *Hadyat al-Shi'a* (Gift for the Shiite) and *Fatawa Rashidiya*. He passed away on August 11, 1905.

[6] Mahmud ul Hasan was a son of Deoband and the first graduate of Darul 'Ulum Deoband. He was a gifted teacher whose classes on hadith, it is said, were reminiscent of the gatherings of the Salaf. Politically, he was a staunch opponent of British colonization.

After graduating from Deoband in 1286/1872, he taught the primers of Arabic literature and fiqh in Deoband, but was quickly promoted to lecturer of Bukhari and Muslim, which he taught for the next 40 years. He is the teacher of many of the sons of Deoband: Maulana Ashraf 'Ali Thanawi, Maulana Anwar Shah Kashmiri, Shibbir Ahmad 'Uthmani, Hussayn Ahmad Madani, Habib ul Rahman 'Uthmani and others. He also played a major role in bringing Darul 'Ulum Deoband to prominence.

He was the embodiment of Shari'a and Tasawwuf and received authorization (khilafat) from both Haji Imdadullah and Maulana Rashid Ahmad Gangohi. His love for his shaykh was so great that he taught his last hadith class in Deoband on Thursday night and then walked 22 miles to Gangoh, stayed with his shaykh, and returned the next day after Jum'ua. His shaykh, Maulana Rashid Ahmad Gangohi, said, "He is the epitome of knowledge," and Hakim ul umma dubbed him the 'Shaykh of the World.' Maulana Shibbir Ahmad 'Uthmani called him

"The Shoreless Ocean of Knowledge."

Another page of his illustrious life was his struggle to liberate the Subcontinent from the British yoke. He masterminded the Silk Handkerchief Plot, which led to his arrest in Makka Mukarrama by the British ally, the Sharif of Makka Mukarrama. The British confined him to Malta from 1917-1920. During the harsh confinement, he wrote his brilliant tafsir of Qur'an, Tafsir 'Uthmani, that was left unfinished upon his death in 1921 (but was completed posthumously by his student, Maulana Shibbir Ahmad 'Uthmani).

[7] Muhammad Yahya Kandhelawi (1871-1917) is another son of Deoband who was a descendant of Abu Bakr 🙏 and the father of the author, Shaykh ul Hadith Muhammad Zakariyya. He was a precocious child, memorizing Qur'an at the age of six and reciting one Qur'an every day for six months onward [approximately 464 Qur'an]. Thereafter, he never opened the mus-haf throughout his life, except once. His memorization was superb and he was known to multitask while reciting Qur'an. After studying the primers of Arabic under his father and mastering the Arabic language, he departed for Gangoh and studied the six books of hadith under the ailing Maulana Rashid Gangoh, took bay'a with him, and served him for the next 12 years until his death. Thereafter, he took bay'a with Maulana Khalil Ahmad Saharanpuri and received khilafat from him. He would transcribe his shaykh's Urdu lectures on hadith in Arabic.

As a brilliant educator of the Islamic sciences, he opposed the one-size-fits-all grading system in traditional madrasas. He preferred an approach that tailored to the individual capabilities of each student. This is how he was able to pick up on great talent and produce great personalities such as his son who became the most eminent muhaddith of his time and Maulana 'Abdullah Gangohi, the commentator of *Ikmal ul Shiyam*.

He privately tutored students, but also taught in Mazahir ul 'Ulum as a substitute for his shaykh; however, he refused any compensation for his services. He made a modest living as a bookseller and printer.

[8] Roti another name for chapatti, a thin-baked bread cooked on a griddle. Here, roti is a metaphor for sustenance.

[9] A political party which called for a separate homeland for the Muslims in the Subcontinent.

[10] Maulana Ashraf 'Ali Thanawi was the imam of Tasawwuf, a prolific author who wrote nearly a 1000 books on varying subjects and sciences. He was also a mufassir and a jurist. He was born in Thana Bavan, U.P, India in 1863-4 and was a descendant of 'Umar al-Faruq 🙏. His father, a wealthy landowner, raised him and his siblings by himself after his mother passed away when he was a child. He was from the first batch of students to graduate from Darul 'Ulum Deoband and his *jalsa* (convocation ceremony), which was the first to be held by Darul 'Ulum Deoband in 1883, was attended by Maulana Rashid Ahmad Gangohi who wrapped the turban around his head.

He studied under the greatest scholars of his time including Maulana Ya'qub Nanautawi, Maulana Qasim Nanautawi, and Shaykh ul Hind Mahmud ul Hasan. He received khilafat in Tasawwuf from Haji Imdadullah. Altogether, he was an embodiment of the best of the shuyukh of Deoband in both Shari'a and Tasawwuf. After graduating, he came to Kanpur and taught in the madrasa, Fayd

'Am for 14 years. His shaykh predicted, "When your heart despairs in Kanpur, return to Thana Bavan and put your reliance on Allah." Maulana Thanawi was shocked since the community at Kanpur adored him, but it so happened that his heart eventually became despondent. Thereafter, he returned to his hometown of Thana Bavan where he reestablished the khanqah of the pious triad (Hafiz Zamin, Maulana Muhammad Thanawi, and Haji Imdadullah) and revived true Tasawwuf in accordance to the Qur'an and Sunna.

To its Subcontinental adherents, Tasawwuf was an unstructured religion that closely resembled the orientalist version of mysticism with no base in any framework of law. It became a brand of Islam that constituted a jumble of rituals and innovations complete with its own class of priests (*pirs*) and a pantheist doctrine. This new brand of Islam resonated with liberals and modernists who wanted to identify with Islam and yet remain unrestrained by its Law. The term Sufism makes many cringe for the same reason, but it also illustrates the dominance of this brand, which conquered the Subcontinent and continues to be imported through celebratory rituals and festivals. At the time, it also received the blessings of the British Raj, who wanted to create illusions of Islam to mislead and divide the masses. In the midst of such turmoil, the khanqah of Thana Bavan became the turning point for reformation and revival of Tasawwuf. Maulana Thanawi revealed its true meaning, purpose, and its methodology while disproving and denouncing the pseudo-Tasawwuf dominating the Subcontinent. He once explained the essence and purpose of Tasawwuf, "To create in Muslims the inner state of the Sahaba ⬥." Highlighting the importance of Tasawwuf as a major component of Islam, he once said, "The Shari'a is the *only* guarantor of all worldly and eternal and outward and inward felicity." He explained that Tasawwuf, as a discipline, was more than just a daily run of dhikr litanies and spiritual exercises. It was about attaining consciousness of Allah in fulfilling rights and saving others from one's harm. His khanqah was a training center for imbibing oneself with humanity. As he once said, "I don't wish to make my gatherings the gatherings of *buzurghs* (shaykhs) but rather, the gathering of true servants," and "I always say that it is easy to become a Shah sahib (honorable title), *Malik ul tujjar* (king of businessmen), buzurgh, or a *Qutb* (Pole), but to imbibe humanity is the toughest thing…you want to become a buzurgh, a wali, or a qutb then go elsewhere, but if you want humanness, then I make humans here."

For all his works, the most famous is the *Bahishti Zewar* (Heavenly Ornaments), an exhaustive Hanafi manual for women, which covers the panoply of women-related issues from salat, zakat, to recipes, and homemade remedies to female exemplars and their accomplishments. His *Hayat al-Muslimin,* a guidebook that illustrates how a Muslim should live his/her life according to the Qur'an and Sunna, is another priceless gem of which he said, "I have never believed that any of my books will help me attain salvation except for *Hayat ul Muslimin*; I am hopeful that Allah will save me by this book. It is the fruit of my life and the essence of my lifework." His Malfuzat (Sayings) runs into 23 volumes and his *Khutubat* (Speeches) into 20 volumes.

He passed away on July 19, 1943 at the age of 80. Some of his students and khalifas are Mufti Shafi' (Grand Mufti of Pakistan), Maulana 'Abdul Rahman Kamilpuri (Shaykh ul Hadith of Mazahir ul 'Ulum, Saharanpur), Maulana Shibbir Ahmad,

Maulana Zafar Ahmad 'Uthmani, Maulana Masihullah Khan, Maulana Shah Wasiullah A'zami, Maulana Khayr Muhammad Jalandhari (founder of Madrasa Khayr ul Madaris [Multan, Pakistan]), and Mufti Muhammad Hasan Amritsari (founder of Jami'a Ashrafiyya [Lahore, Pakistan])
Many regard him as the mujaddid of the last century.

[11] Ikmal ul Shiyam is the commentary by Maulana 'Abdullah Gangohi of the Urdu translation by Maulana Khalil Ahmad Saharanpuri of the *al-Hikam* (The Wisdoms) of Ibn Ata'ullah al-Iskandari.

[12] 'Abdullah Gangohi (circa 1881-1921) was a hand-picked student of Maulana Yahya Kandhelawi. At the age of twelve, he regularly attended the masjid where Maulana Yahya Kandhelawi taught Arabic. He caught the eye of Maulana Yahya, who noted his proclivity for the Deen and encouraged him to change his path to religious studies. Maulana Yahya mentored him and finally placed Maulana Abdullah's hand in the hand of his own shaykh, Maulana Khalil Ahmad Saharanpuri, from whom he finally received khilafat in 1909 (circa). Maulana 'Abdullah used the distinctive teaching method of his mentor, Maulana Yahya Kandhelawi with which he produced two outstanding scholars of the time: Maulana Shibbir Ahmad 'Uthmani, Grand Mufti of Pakistan and the author of *Fath ul Mulhim* (commentary of Sahih Muslim) and Maulana Zafar Ahmad 'Uthmani, the author of *I'la' ul Sunnan*, the collection of Hanafi evidences in 22 volumes.
He taught for the remainder of his life at the local madrasa in Kandhela until his death on the 21st of March, 1921. He is buried in the ancestral cemetery of Shaykh ul Hadith Muhammad Zakariyya.

[13] Miskhat al-Masabih is a famous hadith collection by Allama Abu 'Abdullah Waliuddin al-Tabrizi (d.741/1340), which is a completion of Allama Baghawi's unfinished collection of hadith, Masabih al-Sunna.

[14] One sa'a is approximately three quarts.

[15] Bukhari and Muslim

[16] In Islamic jurisprudence, *sarf* are the laws that regulate bartering, exchanging, or transacting of silver/ gold with silver/gold.

[17] Majmu' al-Fatawa, *Fadl wa hadha al-hadith lahu turuqun 'adida*

[18] Sa'id bin al-Musayyab (16/637-93/716) was a Sufi known for his taqwa and abstinence and also a top faqih who earned himself the title of *Faqih al-Fuqaha* (Jurist of all Jurists). His grandfather was the Sahabi, Hazan bin Abi Wahab al-Makhzumi ﷺ from the Quraysh. Qasim bin Muhammad, one of the seven jurists of Madina Munawwara, said, "He is blessed with the greatest acuity and is the best of all of us." Makhul said, "In my quest for knowledge, I haven't found anyone more knowledgeable than Sa'id bin al-Musayyab." He was authorized to issue fatwa in the lifetime of many great Sahaba ﷺ. Ibn 'Umar ﷺ said of him, "If the Prophet ﷺ had ever seen him, he would be elated." He never missed congregational prayers for 40 years and said, "I have not seen the napes of congregants for 50 years (i.e. he always stood in the front row)." He was flogged and imprisoned for his refusal to take bay'a with the Umayyad king 'Abdul Malik. He was married to the daughter of Abu Hurayra ﷺ.

[19] Shaykh 'Abdul Qadir Jaylani (1077-1166) was a descendant of Hasan ﷺ and one of the most eminent shayukh of Tasawwuf. A jurist, ascetic, and founder of

the Qadiriyya Order, he expounded upon many intricate matters of faith in his sermons and discourses. He is prominently mentioned, defended, and lauded by all the scholars of Ahl Sunna wal Jama'a, including Ibn Taymiyya, Ibn Rajab, Ibn Kathir, Ibn al-Najjar, Ibn Qudama, Ibn Hajar al-'Asqalani, al-Zarkali, al-Manawi, and Imam al-Nawawi, who says in *Bustan al-'Arifin,* "We are not informed by the most authentic narrators of the miracles (*karamat*) of the Auliya of anyone who evinced more miracles than the Pole, Shaykh of Baghdad, Muhiyuddin 'Abdul Qadir al-Jaylani, who was the shaykh of the erudite of the Shafi'yya and Hanabila school in Baghdad. He was the acme of knowledge and his illustrious company produced many Auliya. Most of the notable scholars of Iraq originate from him (i.e. in their transmissions); a large group from the highest spiritual stations were his *murids* (disciples), innumerable creation learned with him, and the Ulema and Shuyukh are unanimous about his illustriousness, his exaltedness…" (al-Rifa'i).

Before his arrival in Baghdad, the capitol city was bleeding from the prevalence of corruption, political unrest, bid'a, and sectarianism. His eminence restored peace, eliminated corruption, and rehabilitated the political and social landscape of the city. He was loved by the ministers, elite, laymen, and educated classes alike and regularly enjoined the good and forbade the evil to the viziers and caliph. He revived the Sunna, eliminated the bid'a, and devoted himself to the reformation of his students, producing over 12,000 walis and thousands of scholars in his lifetime. Approximately the same number of Christians and Jews accepted Islam at his hands.

[20] Majmu' al-Fatawa, A'zam al-Wasiyya al-Masih

[21] *Ibid, al-Fana Anwa'un*

[22] A loose-fitting upper garment that is worn by men.

[23] Ibid, *Fasl: al-Fana al-Maujud fi Kalam al-Sufia*

[24] Jami' al-Rasa'il, *Amr al-Jaylani bi al-Fana'*

[25] Madarij al-Salikin, *Murad al-Fana'*

[26] Ibid, *Fasl al-kaba'ir*

[27] Muslim

[28] Muslim

[29] A demonetized unit of currency in British India. The formula was: one *ana* = 1/16 of a rupee, four paisa = one ana, one rupee = 64 paisa.

CHAPTER TWO

[30] Kanz al-'Ummal

[31] Ibn Maja- In this hadith, the Prophet ﷺ is prophesizing the fitna of the *Ahl Qur'an* sect—those who accept the Qur'an but reject the hadith—and their promoting the fallacious belief that the Qur'an is sufficient without the hadith.

[32] *Mursal* is a hadith narrated by a tabi'i from the Prophet ﷺ with omission of the name of the sahabi ؓ from whom he heard the hadith.

[33] i.e. Shaykh ul Hadith draws attention to the fact that we should not judge our relation with Allah by how we are judged by society and should not care if people call us backward or progressive. All that matters is that we adhere to the Sunna of the Prophet ﷺ.

[34] Shaykh Abu Sulayman al-Darani was born in Daria, a suburb of Damascus. He was one of the shuyukh of Tasawwuf, an authority on transcendental realities, and

was known for his *war'a* (spiritual circumspection). He passed away in 215/830.
[35] Junayd bin Muhammad bin al-Junayd, Abul Qasim al-Baghdadi is the Imam of the Sufia and is known as Syed ul Ta'ifa (Leader of the Group). He learned hadith from Uasan bin 'Arafa and others and became a faqih who issued fatwa according to the school of Abu Thaur of Egypt. He sat in the company of the famous Sufi and his maternal uncle, al-Sirri al-Saqati, and also al-Harith bin Asad al-Muhasabi. Ja'far al-Khuldi says, "We have never seen any of our shuyukh who combined both knowledge and spiritual state. If you saw his knowledge, you preferred it over his state, and if you saw his state, you preferred it over his knowledge." His daily routine was 300 rak'a and 3000 tasbih, but this was only when he sat at his store. For stories of his worship, aphorisms, and enlightening sayings, look in *Tabaqat al-Shafi'iyya.* He passed away in 298/911.
[36] Fudayl bin 'Ayad (d.187/803) was a jurist of Kufa, but became most well-known as a great Sufi from among the *zuhhad* (ascetics) whose sayings are preserved in the books of *Riqaq* (collections of sayings to soften the heart). He was born in Samarqand and lived his early life as a dacoit robbing wayfarers and caravans. The turning point, according to some sources, came when he fell in love with a woman and was about to scale the wall of her house when he heard the recitation of the following (translation of the) ayah, *Has the time not come for those who have believed that their hearts should become humbly submissive at the remembrance of Allah and what has come down of the truth* (57:13)? The ayah shook him up. He repented to Allah and returned what he had robbed to its rightful owners, then settled down and lived the rest of his life in Makka Mukarrama.
[37] Sahl bin 'Abdullah al-Tustari was one of the imams of the Sufia known for his asceticism and profound sayings on Tasawwuf. He passed away in 83/ 702.
[38] A customary greeting predominant in certain areas in the Subcontinent.
[39] Anas 🙵 narrates that once it was raining and we were with the Prophet 🙵. The Prophet 🙵 lifted his clothe until he (i.e. his body) became wet with rain. We said, "Prophet, why did you do that?" He replied, "It is a recent creation of Allah (and thus, a source of blessings and mercy)" (Muslim).
[40] Maulana Syed Asghar Hussayn (1877-1945) was a graduate and senior lecturer of hadith at Darul 'Ulum Deoband (1903). He studied under Shaykh ul Hind and was one of his most accomplished students. Mufti Shafi' notes, "He was affectionately known as Miań sahib.... Even today, thousands of student who studied Abu Dawud under him are around...he was reserved and spoke little. His explanation of hadith was short yet comprehensive, such that enlightened the heart and removed all doubts." He received khilafat from Shah 'Abdullah about whom Qari Tayyib said, "When the time came to lay the first brick of Darul 'Ulum Deoband, Maulana Qasim Nanautawi put a condition: the first brick will be laid by a person who has a virgin heart, i.e. even the thought of sin has never crossed his mind in his life. And then he himself took the name of Shah 'Abdullah (aka Shah Munna sahib)." Syed Asghar Hussayn also received khilafat from Haji Imdadullah.

Many stories are told of his simplicity and solicitude. He lived in a slum neighborhood and had to expend large sums every year for the upkeep of his mud-plastered house after the monsoon rains came. After much insistence for him to fortify his house, he finally said, "All the people in my neighborhood are poor. If I rebuild my home with baked bricks, my neighbors will look upon my house and be grieved, and I do not possess enough to rebuild everyone's home." He passed away on January 8, 1945. His last advice was, "No matter how small a Sunna seems, please never ignore it, for Allah loves every Sunna."

[41] Shu'ab al-Iman

[42] A former British coin worth twenty shillings

[43] Maulana Hussayn Ahmad Madani was a lecturer of Bukhari and Muslim in Darul 'Ulum Deoband, but also a political activist who struggled against British colonialism. He was also a founding member of the political party, Jam'iat 'Ulema Islam. He was born in 1879 in Attawa, U.P. India and was a descendant of Hussayn ﷺ. He memorized the first five juz with his mother and completed the rest with his father, who was a khalifa of the great Sufi, Maulana Fadl ul Rahman Ganj Muradabadi.

He arrived in Deoband in 1892 and quickly won the hearts of his teachers with his zeal for *khidma* (serving his teachers). Shaykh ul Hind Mahmud ul Hasan was a senior lecturer of hadith and a round-the-clock political activist with little time on his hands, but he saw promise in his student. Shaykh ul Hind took Maulana Hussayn Ahmad under his wing and cut out time to privately teach him the curricular books. Through Shaykh ul Hind's guidance, he completed the whole curriculum, which consisted of 17 sciences and 67 textbooks, in six years. Maulana Syed Asghar Hussayn, himself a lover and beloved of Shaykh ul Hind, said that none won the heart of Shaykh ul Hind the way Maulana Hussayn Ahmad Madani did.

In 1898, shortly after graduation, his father migrated to Madina Munawwara with family. Before leaving, Shaykh ul Hind advised him to make it a habit throughout his life to hold a *dars* to teach the sacred knowledge. A few days after arrival, he commenced the hadith sessions and soon had the largest gathering in the Haram which earned him the title *Shaykh al-haramin nabawi*. He returned for a short period to India to teach in Darul 'Ulum Deoband in 1908 and then in Calcutta, Bengal, and Silhat. He followed the advice of his beloved teacher to the very end of his life.

He was the most unconventional of scholars. He was a Sufi, a scholar of hadith, and a senior lecturer, a turbaned politician rubbing shoulders with powerful men, and also a revolutionary fighting for an independent India. For many, his political activism, fatwas issued against British imperialism, and contempt of British law, which often landed him in prison, seemed bizarrely incongruent with his dhikr gatherings, seclusion in Ramadan, and his sitting cross-legged on the bare ground while lecturing on hadith at Darul 'Ulum Deoband. But, for many others, his life was only a mirror image of the life of the blessed Prophet.

After independence, the partition between Pakistan and India created a new set of challenges for the Muslims. The Partition had provoked the massacre of millions of Muslims which augured a growing schism between Hindus and Muslims. Maulana Hussayn Ahmad worked on integrating Indian Muslims into the mainstream, strengthening Hindu-Muslim relations, and also garnering support from influential Hindu figures to condemn Hindu zealotry.

In Tasawwuf, Maulana Hussayn Ahmad Madani made bay'a with Maulana Rashid Ahmad Gangohi shortly before his (Maulana Hussayn Ahmad Madani) migration to Hijaz. Sometime later, he received a letter from his shaykh to return to India. He immediately set off for the long voyage and after receiving khilafat a few days later, returned to Hijaz. He passed away in 1958.

44 Shaykh ul Hadith is referring to himself.

45 *Badhl al-Majhud* is the superb commentary of Abu Dawud by Maulana Khalil Ahmad Saharanpuri that runs in 18 volumes. Shaykh ul Hadith gathered the necessary material and transcribed the commentary of the hadith fror his shaykh.

46 The hadith of naza'ir narrates the order of Suras of Qur'an according to the Mus-haf of 'Abdullah bin Mas'ud ﷺ, which differed greatly from the Mus-haf 'Uthmani (the one we recite today). The shaykh wanted to recite according to the Mus-haf of 'Abdullah bin Mas'ud ﷺ only in tahajjud out of his desire to act upon all the hadith of the Prophet ﷺ.

47 Maulana Khalil Ahmad Saharanpuri was a great Sufi, faqih, and muhaddith of his time, and the author of *Badhl al-Majhud*. He was born in 1852 in Saharanpur, U.P. India. His mother was the daughter of Maulana Mamluk 'Aliyy, the mentor and teacher of Maulana Rashid Ahmad Gangohi and Maulana Qasim Nanautawi. Maulana Mamluk 'Aliyy also performed his *tahnik* (Sunna of placing chewed piece of date in mouth of newborn) and initiated his first reading of the Qur'an. After acquiring basic education in his hometown with his father, he enrolled in Deoband where he studied under his maternal uncle, Maulana Ya'qub Nanautawi and others. Before completing his studies, he returned to Saharanpur and studied in Mazahir ul 'Ulum, Saharanpur under the famous muhaddith, Maulana Mazhar Nanautawi. After completing his studies in 1871, he taught in various places until he was appointed the head lecturer of hadith in Mazahir ul 'Ulum. He taught hadith in Mazahir ul 'Ulum until his migration to Madina Munawwara in 1925. After his first hajj, he received authorization of hadith from Shah 'Abdul Ghani in Madina Munawwara and Shaykh Ahmad Da'lan.

Though a scion of great shuyukh and Sufis, he turned to Maulana Rashid Ahmad Gangohi for bay'a and later received khilafat from him. He was known for his diligence on the daily litanies and devotions throughout his life, no matter his condition or the situation at the time. He memorized Qur'an as an adult and recited Qur'an in tarawih until the last few years of his life. He prayed for three things: 1. Allah bring peace in Hijaz (anarchy prevailed due to the power struggle between the Nejdis and Ottomans). 2. That he complete his commentary of Abu Dawud. 3. That he be buried in proximity to the blessed Prophet ﷺ. All three du'a were fulfilled in his lifetime. He passed away in Madina Munawwara and was buried in Jannat al-Baqi' near the Ahle Bayt in 1927.

He is the mentor and shaykh of Shaykh ul Hadith, Muhammad Zakariyya, his father: Maulana Yahya Kandhelawi, Maulana 'Abdullah Gangohi, the founder of the work of Tabligh: Maulana Ilyas Kandehlawi, and Maulana Badr 'Alam Mirathi: the author of *Tarjuman al-Sunna*, among many others.

48 'Miqdad ﷺ says, "The Prophet ﷺ ordered us to throw dirt on the faces of the praisers" (Muslim).

49 On the morning of the 9th of Dhul Hijja, the haji prays Fajr in Mina and then departs for Arafat. But the mutawwif pressured them to depart before dawn.

50 Shah Isma'il Dehlawi (1779–1831) was the grandson of Shah Waliullah Dehlawi (1703-1762) and a renowned scholar and orator. Shah 'Abdul 'Aziz, the

oldest son of Shah Waliullah, urged him to join the movement of Syed Ahmad Bareli, which aimed at reviving the Sunna and cleansing the Muslim community of the innovations and Hindu customs that had seeped in from the influence of Hindu culture. His oratory was instrumental in bringing thousands back to the Sunna and eradicating innovations from their lives. As the movement grew, Syed Ahmad Bareli took on the expansionist Sikh Empire, which had been persecuting the Muslims of the Punjab. He hoped to gain the support of the Pashtuns and establish his base in the northern region of North-West Khyber Frontier. But the chiefs of the Pashtuns saw their power diminishing with the rise of Syed Ahmad's influence and withdrew their support under various pretexts. When Ranjit Singh's force arrived at Balakot, Syed Ahmad's own army had dwindled to a couple hundred only. After a fierce battle, Syed Ahmad and Shah Isma'il were both martyred on May 6, 1831.

[51] *Arwahe Thalatha, The Three Souls,* is an anthology of the lives of three famous predecessors of the Subcontinent: Syed Ahmad Bareli, Shah Isma'il Bareli, and Maulana 'Abdul Hayy.

[52] Like other masjids from the Mughal era, the Akbari Masjid was built of local sandstone while the floor was unfinished. During the monsoon season, the roof leaked and a section of the masjid floor sunk into the ground.

[53] Lata'if is plural of *latifa*

[54] Ihsan, as narrated in hadith of Jibril ﷺ, is: You worship Allah as if you see Him, and if you cannot, then to be conscious that He is watching you (Bukhari).

[55] *Karima* is an elementary book on the Persian alphabet, while *Bostan* and *Gulistan* are advanced works on Persian literature by Sa'di, the famous poet.

[56] Anglophile historians would like the world to think that the British did a favor by colonizing the Subcontinent, thus, slanting the word from Uprising to Mutiny of 1857. This has been appropriately corrected and renamed the Uprising of 1857.

[57] Allah exemplifies the blessed Prophet ﷺ:
Indeed, In the Messenger of Allah (ﷺ) you have a uswa hasana (**good example**) to follow for he who hopes in meeting with Allah and the Last Day and remembers Allah much (33:21).

[58] After a long journey, the Prophet ﷺ would come to the masjid, pray, meet the people, and then arrive home.

[59] As Abul 'Ala Maududi asserted in his controversial book, *Char Bunyadi Istilahiṅ.*

CHAPTER THREE

[60] Maulana Muhammad Ya'qub Nanautawi was one of the fathers of Deoband, the first head teacher at Darul 'Ulum Deoband, and a clairvoyant Sufi often overcome by *jadhb* (intoxicated spiritual state). A descendant of Abu Bakr ﷺ, he was born in 1834 in the home of Maulana Mamluk ul 'Aliyy, the headmaster of Arab College, who was a teacher of a great many famous men of the time, including Maulana Qasim Nanautawi. Maulana Muhammad Ya'qub and Maulana Qasim accompanied his father to Delhi to study under him (Maulana Rashid Ahmad joined later) in Arab College. He also studied hadith under Shah 'Abdul Ghani and was equal to Maulana Qasim in his grasp of the Islamic sciences. In addition, he was also a lover of knowledge and books and would say, "Even if it may be a

book of profanity, you should read it. If nothing else, you will at least learn two or three unclean words." Once, an Englishman noted his sharpness and offered him the highest-paying job as a deputy collector, but he refused. He was the teacher and mentor of Maulana Ashraf 'Ali Thanawi, Shaykh ul Hind, Maulana Khalil Ahmad Saharanpuri, and many other great scholars of Deoband. His influence over Maulana Ashraf 'Ali, who credited him for his depth of knowledge and cited him frequently, was the greatest. Maulana Ashraf 'Ali said, "I came to him before the graduation ceremony and expressed my shame of being unworthy of receiving any honors at Darul 'Ulum. Maulana responded, 'You say so because you compare yourself to your teachers. When you leave here, *bas tum hi tum ho ge* (there will be none but you everywhere).'" The prediction came true in the lifework and achievements of Maulana Ashraf 'Ali. There are many other stories of his clairvoyance told in *Qisas ul Akabir.*

Though he was a classmate, friend, a relative (i.e. their wives were sisters), and contemporary of Maulana Qasim, he revered him like an elder and wrote a biography on him. He passed away in 1885 and is buried in his hometown of Nanauta.

[61] The first takbir with which the salat is commenced.

[62] Maulana Qari Muhammad Tayyib (1897-1983) was the grandson of Maulana Qasim Nanautawi and son of Hafiz Maulana Muhammad Qasmi, the rector of Darul 'Ulum Deoband for 40 years. He memorized Qur'an at the age of nine under Maulana 'Abdul Wahid Ilahabadi and was a superb reciter of Qur'an. He was a favorite of the teachers, who loved listening to his melodious voice and beautiful recitation of Qur'an, especially in tarawih.

While a student in Darul 'Ulum Deoband, his teachers, Maulana Anwar Shah Kashmiri, Maulana 'Aziz ul Rahman 'Uthmani, Maulana Syed Asghar Husayn Deobandi, and Allama Shibbir Ahmad 'Uthmani all wanted him to take his father and grandfather's place to serve as rector of Darul 'Ulum Deoband, and thus always favored him with their special attention and kind support.

He graduated from Darul 'Ulum Deoband in 1918 and was hired as a teacher soon after. He taught hadith and advanced level subjects to the senior classes. During that same time, noted for his administrative skill, he was appointed as rector of Darul 'Ulum Deoband, a position he held until his death in 1983.

A spellbinding orator from his student days, he was dubbed the Conqueror of Mumbai when his talk in Mumbai to a crowd of 30,000, whose animosity toward the Elders of Deoband was known, won them over. After the talk, he was invited to different masjids for 29 days where thousands of people took bay'a with him. He was fluent in Arabic, Persian, and Urdu, and gave speeches in all three languages.

In 1921, he turned to Shaykh ul Hind for spiritual rectification shortly after Shaykh ul hind returned from Malta. After Shaykh ul Hind passed away, Qari Tayyib turned to Hakim al-umma Maulana Ashraf 'Ali Thanawi who granted him khilafat in 1932.

He was also an author of many books. Among them: *The Philosophy of Salat, History of Darul 'Ulum Deoband, Science and Islam, Faith and Politics,* and *Assimilation and Identity in Islam.* Like his grandfather, he had a philosophical bent which reflected in his writings and discourses.

[63] Caller to adhan

[64] Concession to the number of units in salat for travelers

[65] Maulana Zafar Ahmad 'Uthmani was a muhaddith, faqih, and one of the founders of Pakistan in 1947. He was born in 1893 in Deoband into the 'Uthmani family who are descendants of the third caliph, 'Uthman 🕮. Darul 'Ulum Deoband is built on the plot of land endowed by his grandfather, Nihal Ahmad 'Uthmani. He was also a nephew of Maulana Ashraf 'Ali 'Uthmani who took him under his wing after he completed his elementary studies in Darul 'Ulum Deoband. Hired by Maulana Ashraf 'Ali, his tutor, Maulana 'Abdullah Gangohi, cut and polished this gem into one of the loftiest scholars of the century. His outstanding work, *I'la' al-Sunan*, the ground breaking collection of evidences on the Hanafi school in 22 volumes, exhibited his scholarship in the fields of fiqh, hadith, principle of hadith, and tafsir, and drew acclaim from around the world. The Egyptian scholar, Allama Zahid al-Kauthari, wrote, "The author of *I'la' al-Sunan,* Maulana Zafar Ahmad 'Uthmani, is the hadith master, exegete, researcher, thinker, authenticator, jurist, and great Sufi of the time. I was fascinated by his proficiency and breadth of knowledge. This book is singular in the field of hadith, which is the achievement of this extraordinary scholar, and not a work that can be pulled off by just anyone." Despite being his senior and uncle, Maulana Ashraf 'Ali Thanawi himself was so impressed that he often consulted with him on important matters and said, "Maulana Zafar Ahmad 'Uthmani, who is my sister's son, is the Imam Muhammad of this time and a fountain of knowledge." But, he also drew praise for his noble character and humility. Maulana Khalil Ahmad Saharanpuri said, "Maulana Zafar Ahmad sahib is far beyond in his knowledge and practice; he is the essence of his maternal uncle, Hakim ul Umma Thanawi." Even the imam of Tabligh, Maulana Ilyas, called the attention of the people of Delhi to benefit from his person, to listen to his talks, and sit in his company. He taught in Mazahir ul 'Ulum and Maulana Ashraf 'Ali Thanawi's madrasa in Thana Bavan. Among his students who went on to serve the Deen in different capacities were Maulana Idris Kandhelawi, Maulana 'Abdul Rahman Kamilpuri, Maulana As'adullah Saharanpuri, Shaykh ul Hadith Maulana Muhammad Zakariyya, and Maulana Syed Badre 'Alam Mirati.

He worked hand in hand with the founding father of Pakistan, Muhammad 'Ali Jinnah, to rally the support of the Muslims and educate them about the need for a separate homeland. He was also delegated by Maulana Ashraf 'Ali Thanawi, who had put his weight behind the Muslim League, to support the M.L. He passed away in Karachi, Pakistan on December 8, 1974.

[66] Most likely one of his attendants

CHAPTER FOUR

[67] Gular is the popular Indian name for the fruit that grows from the Indian Fig tree. It is native to Australia, Southeast Asia, and the Indian Subcontinent.

[68] It is customary for people in the Subcontinent to send gifts of food and meals to the elders and shaykhs to receive their du'a and blessings.

[69] A meal after sunset to break the fast

[70] Pre-dawn meal

[71] A little sarcasm by Shaykh ul Hadith. By 'fortunes,' he means the monetary

gifts Maulana Hussayn Madani received from the hosts who invited him for talks.
[72] Since the profit from the money order went to the British Raj
[73] Mawalat is a broad legal term that defines:
1. The protection that a Muslim citizen grants a non-Muslim in an Islamic Republic and the legal code of rights that follow between the two.
2. In the early caliphal conquests, if the conquered accepted Islam at the hands of the conqueror or was freed by him, a code of mutual rights (*wala'*) was established between both parties. Some aspects of the wala' are mandated by the Shari'a, while many others are mutually negotiated between both parties.
Maulana Hussayn Ahmad boycotted British-manufactured products and issued a strict fatwa against any trade that profited British rule. Here, Shaykh ul Hadith is teasing Maulana Hussayn Ahmad, saying in effect that if you do not acknowledge the legitimacy of British rule, then there is no mawalat between you and them, which means they have no legal right to profit from your personal transactions. If they do, mawalat is established, which legitimizes their rule. By purchasing a money order, the their rule is legitimized since a portion of the profits from the sale of a money order go to the British Raj.
[74] A biography on the life of Shaykh al-Islam Maulana Hussayn Ahmad Madani
[75] Look in endnote under biographical account of Maulana Ashraf 'Ali Thanawi.
[76] Maulana Yahya did this to help people out from which he made no profit.
[77] The Pole of the Poles, Haji Imdadullah Muhajir Makki, was the shaykh of shuyukh and spiritual mentor of the elders of Deoband. He was born in Nanauta in 1814 and was named Imdadullah by Shah Ishaq Muhaddith Dehlawi. He completed his memorization at an early age and left for Delhi with Maulana Mamluk al-'Aliyy to study books of the *dars e nizami,* but his natural propensity for Tasawwuf pulled him the other way and he was unable to complete the course. By the age of 18, he had already received khilafat from Maulana Nasiruddin Naqshbandi Dehlawi, and after he passed away, from Mian Ji Nur Muhammad. He migrated to Makka Mukarrama in 1857 and passed away in 1899. He is buried in the graveyard of Jannat al-Mu'alla in Makka Mukarrama.
[78] Khawaja Mu'inuddin Chishti was the founder of the Chishti order (to which most of the Elders of Deoband belonged) and is looked upon as the Imam of Tasawwuf of the Subcontinent since the Chishti order originated and spread mostly throughout the Subcontinent. He was a mujtahid of Tasawwuf and also a great scholar of the sacred law. He taught that Deen is the composite of both the sacred law, which concerns itself with the physical realm, and the esoteric knowledge, which focuses on the heart and its spiritual states.
It is narrated that once, he forgot to make *khilal* (the Sunna of interlocking the fingers in wudu) while making wudu. A voice from the Unseen reprimanded him, "You claim love for the Prophet ﷺ but abandon his Sunna." He immediately repented. Thereafter, whenever he saw a fire, he would shudder out of fear that he may be punished for omitting a Sunna from wudu. His fear after missing the Sunna of wudu highlights his loftiness in Tasawwuf, while his knowledge of the Sunna of wudu illustrates his strict adherence to the sacred law.
Born in 537/1143, he first came to Samarqand, memorized Qur'an, and acquired the sacred knowledge from the scholars of Samarqand. Thereafter, he turned his attention to purification of the heart and came to the village of Harun in Iraq.

There, he took bay'a with Khawaja 'Uthman al-Haruni and served him for the next twenty years. After receiving khilafat, his shaykh departed for hajj and left him with instructions to make the Subcontinent the locus of his mission. He came to Ajmer and made it his capital for the work of Tasawwuf, which continued to the end of his life in 636/1239. He is buried in Ajmer, India.

The excellence of his lofty states and the stories behind his karamat are mentioned at length in the books, but the most impeccable quality of any true follower of the blessed Prophet ﷺ is good conduct. In this respect, he was exemplary. Khawaja Qutbuddin narrates, "I lived in his service for twenty years. He never refused anyone. Whoever came begging, he would slip his hand under the prayer mat and handed the mendicant whatever was destined for him." Also, "In twenty years, I never saw Hazrat get angry even once."

[79] Maulana Yahya, who studied under Maulana Rashid Ahmad Gangohi, may have inherited the chit from his teacher, but like his selfless teacher, he was washed spot-clean of love for the material life and was not in the slightest interested about the chit.

[80] i.e. the chit, which contained the ancient, coveted formula that transmuted herbs and plants into gold. The chit was given to Maulana Rashid Ahmad by one of the roadside, fakir alchemists of Delhi.

[81] Steel trunks and bundles were the closets and storage space of the time where tr extra clothes, belongings, and other house articles were stored. Hazrat possessed neither since he had nothing to store.

[82] A loose-fitting collarless shirt, generally of knee-length

[83] A three-quarter length tunic or coat worn by men in India

[84] A wraparound garment that overlaps and is tied to the right or left side.

[85] Khudashanasi Mela (Fair of Cognizance of God) also known as Mubahatha Shahjahanpur (The Debate of Shahjahanpur) is a historic debate that took place near the village of Chandpur, a few miles from Shahjahanpur in U.P, India on May 7, 1876. The organizers had fixed the event to fulfill a hidden agenda and gave it the illusion of an interfaith dialogue between Hindus, Muslims, and Christians to exchange views about God and increase their understanding of each others' faith. The sponsor and organizer of the fair, Munshi Pyare Lal Kabir Panthi, was a respected and wealthy Hindu landowner who had come under the spell of a Baptist missionary by the name of Samuel Knowles, a passionate missionary working in the local Chandpur area. Munshi ji was inclined toward Christianity and was using his reputation in the Hindu community to help advance Knowles' missionary work. The Hindus of Chandpur were were suspicious that Munshi ji had converted to Christianity. Though he denied converting to Christianity, he hoped to convince the Hindus by letting them hear the Christian arguments. Invitation to the Muslims was only a front for this agenda.

Samuel Knowles was the keynote Christian speaker for the Christian side while Pundit Dayanand Sarasvati, the founder of Arya Samaj (a radical Hindu missionary group), would represent the Hindu side. For the Muslim side, Maulana Qasim Nanautawi and Maulana Abul Mansur, an experienced debater against Christian missionaries, were not officially invited (as noted by Maulana Manazir Ahsan Gilani, the biographer of Maulana Qasim Nanautawi), but the local Muslim community, foreseeing the danger in the Islamophobe Knowles sent off an urgent telegram for him and Maulana Abul Mansur to attend the dialogue. Whatever the case, the fair started with Knowles spitting venom against Islam. Then, Hindus passed up their turn when Munshi Ji, who never intended the Hindus to take the stage, read out a short Sanskrit riddle and quickly stepped off. Maulana Qasim then came up and mesmerized the mixed crowd for the next three days. The first day, he dismantled Christian arguments and objections against Islam, while on the last two, he articulated rational, profound arguments for the truth of Islam. The Christians admitted defeat and many Hindus accepted Islam. For more details on the debate, read Shaukat 'Ali's, *Mubahatha Shahjahanpur*.

[86] Maulana Qasim abhorred meeting people of high-standing.

[87] A fund that was established to support the Ottomans in their ongoing wars against Russia and other European powers.

[88] The son of a nawab.

[89] Maulana Yusuf Kandhelawi (-1965) was the son of the founder of Tablighi Jama'at, Maulana Ilyas Kandhelawi. He graduated from Mazahir ul 'Ulum in 1935 and returned to Nizamuddin, the world headquarters of Tablighi Jama'at. In 1944, he received khilafat from his father and was appointed dean of Kashif ul 'Ulum, the seminary branch of Nizamuddin. In the beginning, he taught the six books of hadith and showed little interest in the work of tabligh, despite his father's wishes. His outstanding commentary of Imam Tahawi's *Sharah Ma'ani al-Athar*, *Amani al-Ahbar*, was written during this time, which demonstrated his proficiency in hadith and jurisprudence. His greatest contribution to the Umma, however, was his acclaimed book *Hayat al-Sahaba*, the most comprehensive collection of stories of the Sahaba ﷺ, which has been translated in many languages.

After the death of his father, he had a change of heart and dedicated his life to tabligh. During his emirate, the Tablighi Jama'at came out of its Subcontinental base and spread throughout the world, gaining a wide following in all the populous continents.

He died in Lahore, Pakistan of a heart attack in 1965 during one of his tabligh tours.

[90] Maulana In'am ul Hasan Kandhelawi was the Hazrat Ji Thalith, or Third Emir of Tablighi Jama'at, who carried on the work of Tabligh after the death of Maulana Yusuf Kandhelawi in 1965. He was born in 1918 in Kandhela. At an early age, he stayed in the blessed company of Maulana Ilyas, his father's maternal uncle, who brought him along to Delhi and taught him the books of Arabic grammar. He studied in Mazahir ul 'Ulum under Shaykh ul Hadith and graduated with high honors. Maulana In'am did not gain due recognition as an eminent scholar because of his work in Tabligh, but Shaykh ul Hadith often consulted with him and trusted his analysis of hadith-related issues. Later, when the seminary branch of Nizamuddin, Kashif ul 'Ulum introduced the final year of *daura hadith* into their course, Maulana In'am was appointed as lecturer of Bukhari where he taught Bukhari for the next twelve years. He says, "I have read *'Umdat al-Qari* and *Fath al-Bari* five times and *Fatawa 'Alamgiri* two times…"

The shift from hadith studies toward Tabligh started with the seed that was laid by Maulana Ilyas in his early days. That seed developed into a perpetual state of grief over the condition of the Umma. His hundreds of tabligh tours to remote villages, Indian hinterlands, and waterless, desolate areas of Muslim population, were beset by enormous challenges that could only be overcome by one whose heart knew no bounds in its love for the Umma. That love was reciprocated on his death on June 10, 1995. People flocked from every part of India while chartered planes flew in from Britain, Saudi Arabia, South Africa, Pakistan, Bangladesh and many other countries to pay their last respects. A half a million mourners attended his funeral prayer. He is buried in Nizamuddin next to Maulana Yusuf Kandhelawi.

[91] To go hungry due to lack of food and drink

[92] Mazahir ul 'Ulum is a prestigious Islamic seminary founded six months after Darul 'Ulum Deoband in 1867 in the northern city of Saharanpur in the central state of Uttar Pradesh (U.P.).

[93] Many of the tree boughs and flotsam drift away in the rivers- Zakariyya

[94] Maulana Shaykh 'Abdul Qadir Raipuri (1878-1962) was blessed with a magnetic spirituality that drew many of the great shuyukh, scholars, writers, politicians, speakers, and other notable personalities of his time to him. The founder of the global Tablighi Jama'at, Maulana Ilyas Kandhelawi, often came to stay in his khanqah for days at a time to 'reset' himself after his 40 day propagative outings. After memorizing Qur'an in his birthplace of Dhudian (Sargodha District, Punjab, Pakistan), he traveled in the tradition of the Salaf, seeking knowledge of Deen from different places. He covered most of his travels (hundreds of miles) by foot and never complained of his hunger and destitution to family and friends. He says, "On my trip from Rampur to Delhi (120 miles), I had only an *akanni* on me, which I gave to the boat operator to cross the river."

After acquiring excellence in hadith, Islamic jurisprudence, logic, and philosophy, he taught in Bareilly and other towns but always felt a spiritual calling.

Like Imam Ghazali, he finally set off on the spiritual voyage that took him through many cities, towns, and villages, searching tirelessly for a spiritual guide to help him see through the meaning of life. He achieved his spiritual aspirations with Maulana Shah 'Abdul Rahim, whom he served for the next 14 years until his passing away. His spiritual struggles during these years, surviving on tree leaves and rolling himself up in the straw mats laid out in the masjid for warmth in the winter, were reminiscent of the harsh spiritual exertions Sufis endured in the past to attain spiritual rectification.

His shaykh bestowed him with the khilafat and said, "Hereupon, know that any thought that crosses your mind is from Allah," and ordered one of his wealthy devotees to build a small house in Raipur in his name. After his shaykh's death, he traveled around Punjab and came to Raipur if only to stifle the memories of his shaykh. He had no intention to settle down in Raipur but his shaykh's foresight proved correct and on one of his visits to Raipur, he stayed for longer than usual. People started coming, the gatherings grew, and he stayed for the next 45 years.

[95] Also known as *zawiyah* in the Arab world, a Sufi cloister for the dhikr of Allah.

[96] The most populous state in India, lying in north-central India; New Delhi, the capital, and the historic Taj Mahal are both located in this state.

[97] Punjab is a province that was divided after the India-Pakistan partition into East and West Punjab respectively. Punjabis are generally regarded as hardy people as indicated in the above anecdote.

[98] Shaykh ul Hadith is referring to an incident from his childhood when his father beat him on the head with a shoe. Reason? He was flaunting a flashy new garment his mother had put on him when his father appeared. The everlasting effect of this beating was that Shaykh ul Hadith developed a lifelong aversion to new clothes and remained ever grateful to his father for it.

CHAPTER FIVE
[99] Maulana Hussayn Ahmad wanted his suhur, the pre-dawn meal, packed so that he could have it on the way. But, Shaykh ul Hadith's wife 'would not take any of that' i.e. she did not accept her guest leaving the house on an empty stomach and woke early to prepare his suhur.

[100] i.e. If she wishes to serve you at suhur, I will not prevent her from doing so.

[101] These were his closest disciples and scholars who could relate to his discourses on the deeper meanings of Tasawwuf.

[102] Hafiz Zamin Shahid was the khalifa of Miań Ji Nur Muhammad, the shaykh of Haji Imdadullah. Haji Imdadullah, Hafiz Zamin, and Maulana Muhammad Thanawi were the spiritual progenitors of Deoband. They established a khanqah in Thana Bavan, which fell into disrepair after the Uprising of 1857 and was revived years later by Maulana Ashraf 'Ali Thanawi.

Hafiz Zamin had a humorous side to him. Once, he gestured to a newcomer to come to him and said, "If you are in need of fatwa, go to the big Maulana over there [pointing toward Maulana Muhammad]; if you want to make bay'a, Haji sahib is sitting right over there; and if you want to smoke a hookah, then come and hang out with your good friend [himself].

He was killed in the Uprising of 1857 against the British. He had cautioned Maulana Rashid Ahmad Gangohi, then a young man, that he might be martyred and had even bathed and dressed for the occasion with new, white clothes. Maulana Rashid Ahmad carried him off the field and into a nearby masjid after he was shot, and there he died in his arms.

[103] Shaykh's monumental commentary of Abu Dawud in eighteen volumes

[104] Though Shaykh ul Hadith himself is the narrator, he uses the third-person for himself, most likely because he was averse to using the word 'I,' which stinks of the individualism that was so repugnant to our Akabir.

[105] In the earlier days, the Saudi Kingdom employed the lunar calendar as its official time format. According to the lunar calendar, a new day begins at sunset which was equivalent to 12 a.m. and thus 8 a.m. corresponds to 2-3 a.m. (GMT), which was the time Hazrat woke up for tahajjud.

[106] The most authoritative book on the history of Madina Munawwara by Nuruddin Abul Hassan al-Samhudi (d. 911/1505).

[107] Plural of hafiz

[108] Maulana Shah 'Abdul Rahim Raipuri (1853-1919) was one of the highest-ranking khalifas of Maulana Rashid Ahmad Gangohi and a great lover of the recitation of Qur'an.

His life started in the small town of Raipur in East Punjab (now a part of India). His father, Rao Ashraf 'Ali Khan, was a wealthy land owner and supporter of Haji Imdadullah. After the Uprising, the Raj indicted Haji Imdadullah and warned that anyone who sheltered him would be executed. Still, when Haji Imdadullah migrated to Makka, he stayed at Maulana Shah 'Abd al-Rahim's father's residence. At the time, Maulana 'Abdul Rahim Raipuri was only 2-3 years old, but he remembers Haji Imdadullah patting his head and making du'a for him.

After completing his Islamic studies in Mazahir ul Ulum, Saharanpur, his love for Tasawwuf and awe for the Deoband shuyukh, whom he loved after hearing their countless stories in childhood, attracted him to the gathering of Maulana Rashid Ahmad Gangohi. After making bay'a with him, his love for his shaykh, devotion to the dhikr, and achievement of ihsan earned him the khilafat from his shaykh soon after.

His love for Qur'an was unrivaled. He set up numerous *maktabs* in his region for teaching Qur'an to children and built a small full-time madrasa on his own land, which also provided students with daily meals. He would enjoy hearing the sounds of their recitation throughout the night and day. This madrasa ran purely on the reliance on Allah without any fundraising or endowments.

Due to his intense devotion to recitation of Qur'an in Ramadan, all meetings and gatherings, public and private, were terminated in the holy month. Though he generally stayed clear of politics, he served as a secret agent in Shaykh ul Hind's clandestine network (Silk Handkerchief Plot) to overthrow the British Raj. Maulana Shaykh 'Abdul Qadir Raipuri [next footnote] was his main khalifa.

[109] The Muhammadan Reality is a teleological account raised by many Sufis to help explain the cause of creation of this world. In summary, they say that Allah brought this world into existence to manifest His attributes and since the blessed Prophet ﷺ was the most complete manifestation of those attributes, he was the cause for this world coming into existence. It should be noted that the M.R. is a metaphysical argument that some Sufis relate through their transcendental experiences and has nothing to do with doctrine.

[110] Shaykh ul Hadith is referring to himself.

[111] Congress was a political party formed in pre-partition India that comprised of many revolutionists who were instrumental in the independence of India. Included in its ranks were Nehru Gandhi, the first prime minister of India, and other prominent figures in Indian history. As one of the founding fathers of India, Maulana Hussayn was well-respected by Hindus, Sikhs, and Muslims alike. He used his weight to advocate for Muslim causes and was key to saving the lives of millions of Muslims during the breakout of violence against Muslims during the partition between Pakistan and India.

[112] By work, Shaykh ul Hadith means that Haji Imdadullah granted Maulana Hussayn Ahmad with the mantle of khilafat. It was therefore his duty to accept disciples into the Order and guide them on the path to purification of heart. Shaykh ul Hadith was objecting to Maulana Hussayn Ahmad's involvement in politics and ignoring the major task entrusted to him by his Shuyukh who granted him khilafat and wanted him to spread the dhikr of Allah.

CHAPTER SIX

[113] Due to his chronic illness, Maulana 'Abdul Qadir could not fast in Ramadan in the last few years of his life. Shaykh ul Hadith is saying that if this is his state (the effulgence of light) when he is not fasting, one can only imagine what it would be like if he had been.

[114] Maulana Abul Nasr saw what few people could see of the exquisite spiritual qualities in Maulana Rashid Ahmad Gangohi and thus loved him dearly. He was his permanent attendant and stayed by his side wherever he went. Maulana Rashid Ahmad caught dysentery on one of the voyages back from Hajj. Maulana Abul Nasr took care of him so well that Maulana Rashid Ahmad Gangohi would say, "He is a mother to me."

[115] Maulana Rashid Ahmad Gangohi was of a quiet nature, which is why few people realized his true status. Maulana Qasim and Maulana Ya'qub, on the other hand, intermingled with people and thus gained a reputation for being saints.

[116] Ticket lanes at the port were similar to airline counters today where baggage is checked in and boarding passes are issued. Likewise, until ticket lanes did not open, hajis could not board a docked ship, even if it was ready for boarding.

[117] Measures were taken at each port of entry and departure to ensure that all pilgrims are free of health issues. Health inspectors boarded the ships and randomly did check-ups on the passengers. If any person/persons were diagnosed with a contagious or infectious disease, the ship would be quarantined and all passengers forced to disembark until clearance was given. Otherwise, they were refused entry and forced to return to their respective countries. Some ports, like the port of Kamran had enforced quarantine on passengers from the Subcontinent due to health-related concerns.

[118] The British Raj had an arrest warrant on him and posted a bounty on his head for his seeking to subvert the Raj after the Sepoy uprising of 1857.

[119] Maulvi Fadil was the title of a scholar who received an Islamic studies degree in the British educational system.

[120] Shah 'Abdul Ghani al-Mujaddidi Dehlawi was a grandmaster of hadith and a teacher for many of the greatest scholars and muhaddithun in the Subcontinent. He was born in 1819 in Delhi, India. His father, Shah Abu Sa'id, was the khalifa of Shah Ghulam 'Ali Mujaddidi from the Naqshbandi order. He was the student of Shah Ishaq Dehlawi in hadith but also received authorization from Shaykh Muhammad 'Abid Sindhi and Abu Zahid Isma'il bin Idris al-Rumi in Hijaz. Upon his return to the Subcontinent, he took up the seat of his teacher Shah Ishaq Dehlawi after he (Shah Ishaq Dehlawi) migrated to Madina Munawwara and commenced his lectures on hadith. Among his students are Maulana Qasim Nanautawi, Maulana Rashid Ahmad Gangohi, and Maulana Ya'qub Nanautawi.
He migrated to Madina Munawwara in 1857, passed away in 1878, and was laid to rest in Jannat al-Baqi'. Both the Arab and non-Arab world are united on his piety and scholarship.

[121] C.U.P was a group of former military officers from the disbanded Ottoman army, which overthrew the Sultanate of the Ottoman Empire and founded their own party on the platform of Ottoman nationalism. The party did not last and was dissolved after World War I.

[122] Lentils and rice mixed into a pudding-like consistency to administer to the sick.

[123] Maulana Muhibuddin had accurately prophesized the bedouin uprising against the Ottomans and the resulting chaos in the Arabian Peninsula, which broke out in 1915-16. The bedouin uprising was orchestrated by T.B. Lawrence (aka Lawrence of Arabia). He stoked the fire of nationalism to create discord and

shatter the unity of the Umma.

[124] Port of departure for hajis at the time

[125] The allusion being made by Shaykh ul Hadith is that Maulana Khalil Ahmad Saharanpuri frequently visited Baqi' to impress upon his attendants and companions that his final resting place will be Madina Munawwara and that they should return to the Subcontinent without him.

[126] This letter was most difficult to translate because it conveys the impassioned mood of its author, Maulana Hussayn Ahmad Madani. It contains streams and streams of prosodic verse from the divans of the Arabic, Urdu, and Persian languages, little of which can be translated without its essence and thrust being lost. This is why I have chosen not to translate most of the poetry and hope expectant readers will forgive me-translator

[127] This letter is a response to a disciple of Maulana Hussayn Ahmad Madani who writes to him seeking advice about going for hajj. It seems that the disciple has also expressed consternation about the voyage and tribulations he may face on the way. The shaykh advises him by reminding him that this is a trip of love in which the desire must be squashed and tribulations must be faced with resolution. He also advises him to meet some of the Elders in the holy cities and offers the assistance of his two brothers in Madina Munawwara if the disciple is ever in need. Shaykh also makes a point of comparing hajj to the other pillars to describe its significance and how it consists of both the attributes of jalal and jamal.

[128] In other words, it is not the harasser or the cause of distress that disturbs your reality but Allah who pulls the strings behind the scenes to test your love for Him.

[129] Majnun and Layla is the epic story of love between Majnun, the lover, and Layla, the beloved. The love of Majnun is often cited in Sufi poetry and writings as a metaphor to emphasize the importance of 'ishq haqiqi (true love) for Allah and how it must transcend love for all creation.

[130] Maulana 'Abdul Bari Nadwi (1886-1976) was the khalifa of Maulana Ashraf 'Ali Thanawi. He was also a beloved student of the famed Allama Shibli Nu'mani who supported Maulana 'Abdul Bari Nadwi despite his father's protests to further studies in philosophy. When Maulana 'Abdul Bari Nadwi's father refused to pay for his tuition fees, Allama Shibli Nu'mani obtained a monthly stipend to fund his education.

Initially, he took bay'a with Maulana Hussayn Ahmad Madani but eventually turned to Maulana Ashraf 'Ali Thanawi for his spiritual needs. He was a professor and head of the philosophy department at Osmania University in Hyderabad, India and translated many of the works of occidental philosophers that were later introduced into the philosophy curriculum. His group of friends included intellectuals like Syed Sulayman Nadwi, 'Abdul Majid Daryabadi (who had introduced him to Maulana Ashraf 'Ali Thanawi), and Maulana Manazir Ahsan Gilani. He passed away in Lucknow, India in 1976.

CHAPTER SEVEN

[131] Al-Durr al-Manthur 6/96

[132] Hayat al-Sahaba ﷺ, 3/396

[133] Maulana Ashraf 'Ali Thanawi borrowed the word *matlun* from the hadith, "The deferring of payment of debt (matlun) is a form of *zulm* (oppression)" (Bukhari),

to indicate that this is a secondary form of aiding and abetting oppression.

[134] He not only taught the six books but also paid for the food and lodging of his 50-60 students. Many wealthy patrons sponsored students or sent money orders for their expenses.

[135] Maulana Ashraf 'Ali Thanawi may have mentioned some of his spiritual states to which Maulana Rashid Ahmad Gangohi responded in this manner.

[136] Maulana Ahmad 'Ali Saharanpuri (1810-1879) was an illustrious muhaddith and jurist of his time. He studied hadith under Maulana Mamluk 'Aliyy Nanautawi and the six books of hadith under Shah Ishaq Dehlawi in Hijaz after completing his hajj. Thereafter, he devoted his life to lecturing on the six books of hadith and worked ten years to revise the manuscripts of Bukhari. He then published the revised edition and wrote a compendious annotation to it. In his last years, he was a lecturer of hadith in Mazahir ul 'Ulum and taught without pay. Among his top students are Maulana Qasim Nanautawi, Maulana Muhammad 'Ali Maungeri, and Allama Shibli Nu'mani.

[137] Madrasa Qadim was built in 1912-13. It is the old complex of Mazahir 'Ulum seminary.

[138] 'Cards and envelopes' were the means of correspondence in those days.

[139] Maulana Mazhar Nanautawi was one of the most renowned muhaddith of his time. He was also the Shaykh ul Hadith of Mazahir ul 'Ulum seminary and its *sadr mudarris* (head teacher). He was born in Nanauta in the district (eq. county) of Saharanpur, India in 1816. He completed the standard Islamic curricula with Maulana Mamluk al-'Aliyy and Shah 'Abdul Ghani al-Mujaddidi and studied Bukhari under Shah Ishaq Dehlawi, the grandson of Shah 'Abdul 'Aziz. He taught in Ajmer and Agra for a short time and took up arms against the British in the uprising of 1857. Thereafter, he returned to teaching and found a position in Madrasa 'Arabiyya, founded by the Hanafi jurist Maulana Sa'adat 'Ali. Though he was older than Maulana Rashid Ahmad Gangohi, he took bay'a with him and received khilafat from him some time later. Because of his wide-ranging contributions to the development and expansion of Madrasa 'Arabiyya, it was renamed Mazahir ul 'Ulum after him. He passed away in Saharanpur in 1886.

[140] Maulana Yahya Kandehlawi was the father of Shaykh ul Hadith and the student and khalifa of Maulana Khalil Ahmad Saharanpuri. When Maulana Khalil Ahmad Saharanpuri took a one-year break from the madrasa to stay in Madina Munawwara, he appointed Maulana Yahya to teach in his place. During the one-year hiatus, Maulana Yahya taught in Saharanpur and gave the monthly salary to his shaykh's wife. Maulana Khalil Ahmad Saharanpuri explains above that he (Maulana Khalil) only accepted the salary because of his appointment of Maulana Yahya in his place. Now that Maulana Yahya had passed away and he himself can no longer teach, he is submitting his resignation.

[141] Pan (*pän*) is a stimulant masticatory that is made of crushed betel nuts, lime, and other added flavors and spices wrapped in a betel leaf that is a favorite of many in the Subcontinent.

[142] This anecdote reveals Hazrat's deep level of taqwa. He did not want to use the lantern because he knew the stationmaster was not authorized by its owners (the railway company) to make personal use of it. Since the stationmaster gave it to Hazrat out of respect for him, it was all the more difficult for Hazrat to explain to

him that he could not use it without the stationmaster, who was Hindu, objecting against the Deen.

[143] Only one third of wealth can be willed in a terminal illness. If the attendant had replied yes, Hazrat would further inquire if it was from one third of his wealth or not. The attendant would most likely be ignorant of the matter and the gift would not be accepted.

[144] A huge sum in that time

[145] As an agitator for independence, Hazrat traveled frequently to attend and organize demonstrations, conventions, and protests.

[146] In protest against certain policy changes by the board of Darul 'Ulum Deoband, many senior teachers resigned from the madrasa followed by at least half the student body. Darul 'Ulum Deoband was so shaken by the internal conflict that some feared it would be shut down for good. That is when Maulana Hussayn Ahmad came along. He was offered a senior position as head teacher, which he accepted wholeheartedly on the condition that his political activities will continue as before. This meant, among other things, frequent absences from classes and irregular class times. The board agreed, but those who were unaware of the details of the signed agreement objected to the time he spent away from classes organizing events or in jail for his brushes with the British Raj.

[147] A moderate political party in India

[148] Some of the anti-Congress donors of Darul 'Ulum Deoband objected against Darul 'Ulum for appointing Maulana Hussayn Madani as head teacher and withheld their donations to the madrasa in protest.

[149] The third-class was ridden by indigent passengers who usually reeked of horrible odors.

[150] Instead of naming the route path [e.g. Route 66, Interstate 81], a train was designated by the route it took. So, for example, the Calcutta Mail Train was the train that ran between Calcutta and Sehara.

[151] A province of Pakistan

[152] As many guests and visitors came to Hazrat and gave donations to the madrasa, his stay in the madrasa complex was a windfall for the madrasa.